Two Plays

Marco Micone would like to thank Antonio D'Alfonso and
Serge Hervouet-Zeiber for corrections brought to *Voiceless People*.
The Publisher wishes to thank Mary Williams
for corrections brought to *Addolorata*.
Ms Maurizia Binda and Guernica Editions gratefully
acknowledge financial assistance from the Canada Council
for the translation and publication of these plays.

Original Title:
Gens du silence & Addolorata
Guernica Editions, P.O. Box 633, Station N.D.G.,
Montréal (Québec), Canada H4A 3R1

Legal Deposit — 1st quarter
Bibliothèque nationale du Québec & National Library of Canada.

Canadian Cataloguing in Publication Data
Micone, Marco
Two plays: Voiceless People and Addolorata
(Drama series; 2)
Translations of: Gens du silence and Addolorata.
ISBN 0-919349-71-4 (bound)
ISBN 0-919349-72-2 (pbk.)
I. Title. II. Title: Voiceless People. III. Title: Addolorata.
IV. Title: Gens du silence. English. V. Title: Addolorata. English.
VI. Series
PS8576.I27T96 1988   C842'.54   C88-090067-9
PQ3919.2.M43T96 1988

Contents

Voiceless People

A mio fratello
Michele

If emigration could have helped
the working class to emancipate itself,
it would never have existed.

Immigrants. Who are they? Why are they here? Did they choose to make this their homeland? Youngsters, men and women give their answer. In this way, they break the silence, the silence all too often an accomplice of those who manipulate and exploit them. *Voiceless People* deals with issues that reach all those who, even if they did not emigrate, share the same social conditions as the imported who make up Chiuso (pronounce *Kyouso*). Revolt is in the air. Mario's revolt is like a cloud before the downpour: threatening and impenetrable, whereas Gino's revolt is led in a clearheaded way. For their part, Nancy and Anna unmask the oppressing agent and discover a male behind it. Antonio (the father) is besieged. The male, endowed with privileges, and whose authority had always been unquestioned, seeks refuge in the past, while his wife and daughter state out loud who they are, so that those who feel like them can join them. Antonio feels just as alone as when he had first arrived.

THE CHARACTERS

Antonio	The father
Anna	The mother
Nancy	Their daughter; aged 26 (studied French at McGill)
Mario	Their son; aged 18
Gino	A friend of Nancy; aged 23
Zio	Balloon-man; aged 75 (wearing a multi-colored suit)
Rocco	A friend of Mario
Other People	

The play can be played by six actors.

SCENE ONE

Throughout the first six scenes, the following leitmotif is heard in two or three languages, typical of Quebec immigrants:

Those who have driven us from our land and those who have made outcasts of us here are the same kind of people.

As the light slowly comes on, a figure emerges from a corner of the stage. Antonio enters, carrying a suitcase tied with a rope. He takes a few steps, then stops. Meanwhile, the image of Collina is seen back stage. Collina, a sun-bleached stonehouse village, sits on a hill in Southern Italy.

AN ACTOR

It was a day like any other day.

FIRST ACTOR

Vincenzo.

SECOND ACTOR

Maria.

11

THIRD ACTOR

Franco.

FOURTH ACTOR

Teresa.

FIFTH ACTOR

They all walked down the valley before sunrise.

ALL

It was a day like any other day.

In succession, five actors:

FIRST ACTOR

But all of a sudden...

SECOND ACTOR

All of a sudden, on the horizon...

THIRD ACTOR

The sky...

ALL

The sky...

FOURTH ACTOR

The sky plunged into darkness...

FIFTH ACTOR

And then...

ALL

And then, a dreadful storm arose.

In succession, five actors:

FIRST ACTOR

The children...

SECOND ACTOR

The children sought refuge at their mothers' bosoms.

THIRD ACTOR

The old folks...

FOURTH ACTOR

The old folks moaned like injured animals.

FIFTH ACTOR

While emigrants' work-widows...

ALL

While emigrants' work-widows watched, powerless, their men being taken away like majestic oak. Far, very far away.

The stage dims out slowly.
Chorus exits. Antonio is left alone.

The image of Collina fades as the spotlight picks up Antonio taking a few steps towards the audience. He is wearing a travel-wrinkled suit and carries a suitcase tied with rope. He takes a few steps towards the audience, then remains for a few seconds motionless, looks up high, executes a long sweeping turn that results in slight dizziness as he stares at the high-rise buildings. Suddenly, a car is heard screeching in the street directly beside him. Startled, Antonio turns white, retreats a few steps, sits on his suitcase, eyes aghast. A few seconds later, he fumbles through his pocket, but doesn't seem to find what he is looking for. He then opens his suitcase, removing cheese, salami, wine and clothes. In the dim light, actors are seen but cannot be distinguished. Antonio relives his departure.

ANNA

Don't forget to write, Antonio. Send pictures, lots of pictures for Annunziata. And be careful of the cars. It seems they're everywhere.

Anna cries.

PRIEST

Church bells can be heard feebly in the background.

Don't forget, my son, that everything that happens to men is foreseen by the generous but sometimes inexplicable organization of Providence. Do not forget, my son, the church where you were baptized. The bell-tower, two hundred years old, is a constant threat to your parish brothers. There are almost as many of you there as there are here. A few dollars each will be enough. The Lord is His infinite love opens the doors of abundance, prosperity and happiness to you. Be grateful. May God bless you! Don't forget the bell-tower! How

14

many times have the bells dispersed storms, stopped the hail and saved the crops. If the bell-tower fell, it would be the end of the village. Don't forget.

Pause.

A WOMAN

Stop crying, Anna. Antonio's not going to prison, but to America.

A SECOND WOMAN

You're lucky, Antonio. You're going to eat meat every day. But we, Antonio, are going to continue living as goats.

ANTONIO

At last, he takes out a small harmonica and plays a lively tune, a tarantella dancing away to the music until sheer exhaustion overtakes him. He collapses on his suitcase and plays a melancholy tune. He then shouts two or three times:

Is there anyone in this land?

The stage dims out as Antonio repeats this phrase.

SCENE TWO

*Antonio is wearing work clothes. He is
devouring a huge sandwich. Close to him a
bricklift. Screen image might be used: Antonio's working conditions on a construction site
and his life in the poorer sections in Montreal.
High above the stage, two windows flicker and
go out alternately, as corresponding voices are
heard.*

WOMAN

With Québécois accent.

Every week, they come in by the boatloads. They come
here to take our jobs. That's why there's no work left
for us. There are so many immigrants now that we have
no apartments left for us in our own country. Would
you believe it!

MAN

With Québécois accent.

To top it all, they bring gifts to the boss: wine by the
gallon, salami, just anything. No one kisses an ass better
than them. Considering the salary they make, I'd rather
be on welfare.

16

WOMAN

Fifteen of the buggers pile in the same house. And they eat anything, you know. Dandelion, I swear! I saw them in the park the other day, they picked two bagfuls. Dogs roam all over that park and just do their business anywhere. They're so weird, I swear. They're so weird. I can understand why we don't want them in our schools.

MAN

Those women, they don't walk, they're so fat they waddle! Spaghetti is good, but there's a limit.

WOMAN

In autumn, they can tomatoes for weeks. It just can't be that they eat all that!

MAN

We're being robbed. I'm telling you, we're being robbed. I think they send all that stuff to Italy. Same as for the apartments. Soon there will be no tomatoes left for us either. It's awful!

WOMAN

They're so dirty! Take a look when fat Maria hangs up the laundry. Real bush under her arms!

Whispers.

Come here a second. I want to tell you something. How come their men are so damn good-looking?

Pause.

Honest folks stay home, okay? Just look in *Allo Police*, they always have these immigrants' stories. And they come from everywhere, to top it all. When it's not the Mafia, it's the Sicilians, and when it's not the Sicilians, it's the Italians. They come from the four corners of the world. Now, even the Wops from the States are coming in. Can you tell me why the hell we let them stay if they take everything from us?

MAN

I remember when I was working... There were always five or six of them lined up before the factory holding their oily lunch bags, their suits too tight, their pants too short... wasn't because their legs were too long either. The tallest must have been five feet! Just tall enough to work at the machine. If they had been an inch shorter, they wouldn't have been able to work on the damn machine. Some worked ten hours a day propped on the tip of their toes! That's how short they were. The boss took them just the same, because they wouldn't even go for a leak. They'd work all the time. They never took their break. They would hardly take fifteen minutes for lunch. Sure enough, when the boss started looking my way, I had no choice. If I didn't want to lose my job. I had to do like them. I'd never go for a leak during work. I never took a break, nor at ten, nor at three o'clock. And at lunch, I would eat a huge dandelion and egg sandwich to pick myself up... in five minutes. After a couple of months, I started getting scared. That's when I took off from the factory. They would take me for a real Italian. Me, an Italian! Me! Gosh, my whole family was born here. My wife, my six kids and my eighteen grandchildren. Me, Lorenzo Del Vecchio, an Italian, a Wop? No way, no way!

18

SCENE THREE

Antonio is in bed writing, obviously ill. A dialogue between Antonio and his doctor can be heard when Antonio stops writing.

ANTONIO

You see, Doc... if I had known... she was dressed up like some fine lady! Boots up to her knee — she looked like a real actress.

DOCTOR

They should all be thrown in jail.

ANTONIO

It's not a good idea, Doc. I know quite a few guys who'd follow them to jail.

DOCTOR

We should have tougher laws, but we've got a bunch of spineless jellyfish at City Hall.

ANTONIO

I know they make the best customers!

Pause.

Is it serious, Doc?

DOCTOR

No, but next time, play it safe.

ANTONIO

Play it safe, play it safe! That's expensive you know, Doc. I don't earn what you do. To top it all, I've got a wife and kid back home in Italy.

DOCTOR

In Italy? Oh! Lago Maggiore! Piazza San Marco, the Medici Palazzo! How fortunate you were to have grown up in such grace and culture.

ANTONIO

You know, Doc, I've never even been to those places. Before coming here, I have never travelled abroad.

Antonio quickly finished writing his letter and then reads it out loud. An Italian translation is heard in voice-over. There is a photograph within reach.

"September 30, 1959.
Dear Anna,

With this letter, I am sending you a picture of what I ate last Sunday. Show it to Peppe and Tina and tell them that everyday is Sunday, especially Saturday night.

"I am putting a lot of money aside. I already get sixty dollars a week and I put aside a hundred and twenty in the bank — a hundred and twenty dollars a month.

"My health is fine and I do a lot of overtime. Half for the boss and half for me. Here when a guy works overtime, it means the boss likes him a lot. Since I just got here, I haven't missed a single day at work. Here you don't have to speak the language to be able to work. In fact, my boss would rather have guys just off the boat. Here in Chiuso there's no shortage of them. They land everyday and they're not just from Collina.

I often think about you and Annunziata.''

He takes the picture from his wallet.

"Do you talk to her about me? I don't even recognize her in the last picture. She seems to have grown so much! By the way, don't forget to send two liters of olive oil and some cheese with Cousin Sabino. You wouldn't believe it, but they make oil from corn here. Don't send any sausage this time. It doesn't agree with me anymore. Now the bad news.

"Prime Minister Duplessis just died after a huge party with the Americans. Many are worried because he was a strong man, and he was. They say he liked hardworking people and couldn't stand strikes. Just like back home before the war. Some people even say we'll be sent back. But the owner of the Italian paper and the priests promised they'll stick up for us.

Your husband,
Rossi, Antonio.

P.S. One more thing. When you write the address, don't just write Canada after Montreal; you have to write Quebec.''

SCENE FOUR

Time and place: Antonio's and Anna's home in the early Sixties. Anna is at her sewing machine while Antonio, sitting at a small table, is helping his wife by sticking labels on the clothes.

ANTONIO

I swear, things aren't going too good. Another bomb just went off. Some day, poor innocent people are going get hurt. I wonder what the hell those separatists want.

ANNA

They talk about it on the radio every night. I think they want to separate.

ANTONIO

Anyway, if they go on like this I bet you they'll start getting rid of the big shots... and some will end up leaving like they always do. Because it's always the same whenever something is wrong. We immigrants always get blamed.

ANNA

I don't think anything serious will happen.

ANTONIO

Yes, sure! You women, you women can't see past the tip of your nose. But when the worst happens, who is it that ends up pulling their hair out?

ANNA

You're getting involved in things that don't concern you. We haven't been here that long.

ANTONIO

Maybe you don't think so, but I've been here for four years.

ANNA

We're not at home here. What would you say if the neighbour came in and told us what to do?

ANTONIO

We're all immigrants in this country. And only because they are more of them, it doesn't mean that they should have the right to decide for us.

ANNA

They got here a few years before us too, you know.

ANTONIO

It was an Italian guy who got here before anyone else: Giovanni Caboto.

ANNA

Listen, I didn't come here to talk politics. I came here for our little Annunziata.

ANTONIO

I swear that if there had been bombs earlier, you wouldn't have been here.

ANNA

Annunziata had to see her father.

ANTONIO

Sure, she had to see her father, not all this violence.

ANNA

She doesn't understand what's going on, she's only five.

ANTONIO

Loudly.

But I know what's going on!

ANNA

Antonio, keep it down, you'll wake her up.

ANTONIO

Getting up.

I'm going to bed.

ANNA

I didn't even make five dollars today. We should work another half hour.

ANTONIO

Tell that Jew to give you a raise. I'm not going stay here till midnight, sticking on labels.

24

ANNA

As a matter of fact, last week he told me some Greeks just moved into the neighbourhood. Seems their women do the same work for less money.

ANTONIO

Couldn't they have stayed at home instead of coming here and driving our wages down. All we need now are blacks. What about Concetta? What does she make?

ANNA

Six dollars a day.

ANTONIO

Almost as much as a man! Knowing her, she has her parents working till midnight. I told you to get your parents over here too!

ANNA

My parents will never set foot here. If you really want to know, Concetta makes six dollars a day now because she works at the factory.

ANTONIO

Amazed.

At the factory? Concetta... at the factory?

ANNA

I don't understand why you're looking at me like that! She isn't the only one.

ANTONIO

Go take a look around a factory and you'll see what it's like. It's worse than hell.

ANNA

Can't be worse than here. At least there are people around.

ANTONIO

People and machines everywhere.

ANNA

At least when you're through, you're through.

ANTONIO

Sure, but when you're there, you can't even take a leak when you want to. The boss follows you everywhere.

ANNA

Concetta, she even made some friends since she started working at the factory.

ANTONIO

Sure, friends fill up your head with all sort of ideas. It's not Collina here. It's a big city. There are all kinds of people here. You have to watch out, even with our own people.

Pause.

ANNA

They also say when you're out of work, you can get
unemployment insurance.

ANTONIO

Aggressively.

Unemployment Insurance? There will never be a cent of
Unemployment Insurance in this house. Unemployment
Insurance is for lazy French Canadians, not for us.

Pause.

And tomorrow, I'm having the phone taken out.

*Antonio exits. Anna is left alone to work at
her sewing machine.*

SCENE FIVE

Same set as previous scene. Anna is working at her sewing machine. Antonio and Rocco are playing cards; an Italian newspaper lies open on the table.

ROCCO

Did you see the paper? Seems that there are twice as many unemployed among the immigrants that among the *Canadesi francesi.*

ANTONIO

There's nothing you can do, Rocco. There are winners and there are losers. Hey, I won again!

Loud laugh.

ANNA

You only win at cards. Every other way, you're a loser.

ROCCO

You always have the right cards...

ANTONIO

That's not enough. Doesn't only take aces and kings to

win. You need to know how to play cards. Same as in
life.

ROCCO

You mean that...

> *He gets up to leave, but Antonio holds him*
> *back.*

ANTONIO

Sit down. You didn't get me. I'll give you an example.

ANNA

The English again, right?

ANTONIO

Yes, the English don't only have the right cards, they
also know how to play them. That's why they win. It's
important to understand that.

ANNA

> *Mockingly.*

For our children.

ANTONIO

Yes, for our children. Our kids have to learn to play the
game. They have to learn how to win. That's why we
have to send them to English school.

ANNA

You keep winning because you play the same game over
and over again. Try another game for a change.

ANTONIO

Tell her. Only losers want to change their game, never winners. In America, the English are the big winners, they'll never change the game.

ROCCO

You're right, the bosses are all English.

ANNA

I know one who's not English.

ANTONIO

Who?

ANNA

You!

ANTONIO

Laugh, laugh at me all you want. I'm an immigrant. You can't compare me to the English. I wasn't born here.

ANNA

You simply don't understand.

ANTONIO

Rocco, we have to open our eyes so our kids can have a decent living. Even a blind man can see that *i Canadesi francesi* are worse off than us.

ROCCO

To top it all, they speak so awful. Makes you wonder whether they have a language of their own.

ANTONIO

They're good for nothing, those people. In Collina, has anyone ever heard of Quebec? When the first Italians came to Montreal, it was a village. There wasn't anything here. It's only since we got here that it's become a big city. Remember what we had hanging in the kitchens of Collina beside the crucifix. Lesage?

Laughs.

No way, we had a picture of Roosevelt, the president of the U.S.A. We didn't even have a picture of the Canadian president.

ROCCO

When I first got here, they didn't have the "Britannical" Gardens. We had to go to Jarry Park for our wedding pictures.

ANTONIO

And on top of that, *i Canadesi francesi* are so lazy. They can't get their asses off the ground. Those newspaper people aren't dumb, they went to school. And not just anywhere — in Italy, *Italia!*

ROCCO

Seems there's even a priest involved.

ANTONIO

I don't trust priests when they're delivering their sermons, but when they write in the paper, there's no one more honest.

ROCCO

How do you expect *i Canadesi francesi* to buy a house? When they're not going out to a restaurant, the restaurant comes to them.

ANTONIO

If they only ate good food! Their pizza is as thin as the Holy Host in Church and what's more, it's made by Greeks.

ROCCO

How do you expect them to eat a real crusty pizza? They all have dentures.

Very loud laughs.

Could you imagine yourself with a wife like that?

ANNA

And what about Francine, your sister-in-law?

ROCCO

Francine? My sister-in-law? My brother's wife? True, she's *una Canadese francese,* but she comes from the country just like us. You'd think she's from Collina the way she talks like us. She's got to have Italian blood in her.

ANTONIO

They spend money like water. On Monday mornings they have nothing left for the rest of the week.

ROCCO

Those people spend everything they make. Even Francine is like that. They're always buying something, those people. I don't know if you've noticed, but for Christmas they actually start buying their gifts in October.

ANTONIO

Mockingly, after having spoken to Rocco in a low tone.

For the past two hundred years they keep complaining that they had the wool pulled over the eyes. Don't really know what they're complaining about. If they can pull the wool over *our* eyes, it's because we really are sheep.

ROCCO

The English pull the wool over the eyes of all French Canadians, and we're here to steal their jobs. It's always someone else's fault. What a bunch of cowards!

ANTONIO & ROCCO

Standing facing the audience.

We job-stealers? We job-stealers?

Pause.

ANTONIO

Puts down the argument in a mocking tone.

33

Job-stealers? The *Canadesi francesi*, they're the job-stealers. Yes, they're the ones who take jobs from the immigrants. Otherwise, how could you explain that there are twice as many jobless among the immigrants than among the *Canadesi francesi?*

ANNA

Anyway, if it were possible to steal jobs, I would have stolen a better one.

SCENE SIX

In the darkness we hear repeatedly:

Le Québec aux Québécois!
McGill français!

> *Stage lights up gradually. Only Zio is seen, dressed in a multicoloured suit, holding colourful balloons tied together with long strings.*

ZIO

Balloons, balloons, balloons in all colours. Balloons for all, big and small! Fly away with red ones, green ones, white ones...

> *In the background,* Le Québec aux Québécois!

> *Sarcastically imitating the slogan:*

L'Italie aux Italiens! L'Italie aux Italiens! My grandfather shouted it, gun in hand, more than a hundred years ago. And then, foreign bosses were replaced by Italian ones. Ever since, dozens of Collinas emptied out to make up Chiuso, which is cooped up between three cement quarries and the Metropolitan Boulevard. They provided the cheap labour which the Montreal big shots needed in their factories during the Fifties, just like the Quebec villages had done before them. And while the Québécois were giving birth to St. Henri, Collina was shutting itself away in Chiuso. Chiuso is the silence of a vacuum and the racket of chaos. It's a cry from limbo, neither angel nor devil. It's the voice of the Minotaur, neither man nor beast. It's the forsaken language of the underdog and the uprooted. Chiuso is the stiffled revolt of the man from nowhere. But Chiuso is also the stage where language is the language of the power it seeks. For once, it will neither be misunderstood nor scorned.

Pause.

While Zio exits, the slogan Le Québec aux Québécois *is heard softly. Then, as the light slowly dims, the slogan becomes louder.*

SCENE SEVEN

It is June 1980, St. Anthony's Day. In front of Antonio's white brick house. In the distance, the fascist anthem is played by a local band. Religious anthems may follow. On the balcony, a huge poster of the local candidate in the coming school elections, on which is written Votate. *At hand, a bottle of wine and glasses. Anna is knitting or mending. Gino and Nancy are rereading a text.*

ANTONIO

Rolling a sprig of parsley between his teeth.

What was I telling you... There are more Italians that come to celebrate St. Anthony's than separatists in all of Quebec. If they ever hold another referendum, they're going lose their shirts.

GINO

Whistling — mockingly — a few bars of the anthem that was being played.

The old snoring motherland, with its gang of blackshirts soaked in holy water, remains untouched.

ANTONIO

Swallows the parsley.

If you spoke Latin, I'm sure I'd understand you a lot better. I don't know exactly what you're saying, you poet, but I'm sure you're criticizing the celebration again, even though it's a hundred times better than your boring shows. You're wasting your time, I'm telling you. Last Sunday, there weren't even fifty people at your...

Looking for the word.

NANCY

Symposium.

ANTONIO

Yes, your symposium. Go look in front of the church, there are at least five thousand people. They're all like me: they can hardly spell their names. How do you expect them to understand the stories you find in your books as thick as bricks?

ANNA

Antonio, shut up. They know better than you or me what they have to do.

ANTONIO

Well, you never speak up when we're alone...

ANNA

I can't talk to you!

ANTONIO

But when you daughter is there, there's no stopping
you.

ANNA

You're lucky your nephew is around.

ANTONIO

I get no respect. I get no respect.

ANNA

Respect has to go both ways.

ANTONIO

In a loud voice.

Exactly. When the wife doesn't respect her husband
anymore, how do you expect the kids to respect their
father?

ANNA

Stop shouting, there are people around. You just don't
want to understand.

ANTONIO

What am I supposed to understand? Your stories, or
maybe your daughter's and Gino's?

ANNA

It wouldn't hurt you to listen to them, instead of leaving
once you counted the people attending, like you did last
Sunday.

ANTONIO

I belong to the majority. The majority rules in everything.

NANCY

Why don't you go join your majority at the wrestling match the priest organized?

ANTONIO

Sure thing. I'll never go listen to kids like you that still have their mother's milk running down their chins.

GINO

There's more than just wrestling. There's also a draw for a brand new car, just like the one a nun won last year. You never know, this year it may be your turn...

ANTONIO

It's good-for-nothings like you that count on luck to get what they want. Me, I work to get what I want.

GINO

We've got a surprise for you today, just before the match.

ANTONIO

Loud laugh.

And you think the priests will let you do it?

GINO

Yes, because we're going illustrate a chapter from the Gospel.

ANTONIO

If he lets you in, kiddo, it's because he's setting a trap for you that you don't know about.

To Nancy.

If I see you with him today, you'd better never set foot in here again.

NANCY

I'll do what I feel like, and you're not going stop me.

ANTONIO

To Anna.

Did you hear your daughter? Did you hear the teacher?

To Nancy.

What would you say if one of your pupils spoke to you like that, eh?

NANCY

To get that kind of answer, I'd have to behave like you.

ANTONIO

Just remember that it's because you listened to me that you stayed decent. You should get down on your knees and thank me.

ANTONIO & NANCY

Nancy imitating her father.

You'll be able to go to your husband with your head held high!

NANCY

And I might add: "I am the daughter of Rossi Antonio, virginal, pure, immaculate, like my father wanted me to be."

GINO

Intervenes to defuse the situation.

We're going to put on a play today. People will laugh, they're going to have fun. Nancy won't even be seen. You'll see, it's something for the majority, *your* majority.

ANNA

And the women are going leave just before the wrestling.

NANCY

Just before male vulgarity bathed in holy water makes its appearance.

ANTONIO

Chiuso women like processions. They were all there this morning.

ANNA

I didn't show up.

ANTONIO

Oh, you, since your feet started to swell up, you can't even walk to the bus stop.

ANNA

There are more and more women who have swollen feet, Antonio.

ANTONIO

It's because you don't drink enough wine: wine's the best thing for those roadmaps on your legs. Take it from me.

ANNA

Last Sunday, at the symposium...

ANTONIO

Because you went too?

ANNA

Yes, I went with the women from my factory. Their feet are getting more and more swollen too. Last week, we went to sit on the nice carpet in the Jew's office to get a raise. We didn't get up as long as our feet were still swollen. They'll all be there this afternoon, Antonio, like last Sunday.

ANTONIO

Pointing to Gino and Nancy.

We don't need them. What can they do for us? We need people with influence, people who can get respect and get respect for us, too. I don't need a speech to understand that my boss has a damn good life compared to mine. We need people to defend our homes and make sure there's respect, respect for authority.

43

Pointing at the poster.

GINO

Smiles.

Take him, for example.

ANTONIO

Exactly. He's a real influential man. He's rich, he owns a newpaper, he's got everything to stand up for us.

GINO

Ironical.

Did he get rich by standing up for us? Sure thing!

ANTONIO

If he was smart enough to get rich, he'll be smart enough to speak up for us. It's thanks to him and the priests that immigrants' children can still go to English school.

NANCY

That's what he said in his newspaper, of course. Your candidate and your priests haven't done anything but give people in power a chance to justify a Machiavellian plan they've been working on for a long time. A plan to exclude us, to make us marginal, to stop our emancipation so we can keep being cheap labour longer.

ANTONIO

Beside himself.

Talk so I can understand you.

NANCY

The real English send their kids to French school so that they can stay bosses. It's the phony English like you who don't understand a word of English who send their kids to English school. Your candidate, that hypocrite, that defender of English schools, married a French-speaking Québécois. Do you think she'll let her kids go to an English school?

GINO

Even the priests would send their kids to French school, if they had any.

ANTONIO

America is English.

NANCY

In Collina, do they send the kids to German schools because there's a Germany in Europe?

ANTONIO

You never know. What if there's no work here... and we have to move to Toronto.

ANNA

We're fifty years old, Antonio.

ANTONIO

I'm not speaking for us, dammit, for *her*, for *Mario*.

ANNA

We had no choice, that's why we left.

ANTONIO

They won't have a choice, either. What did Laplante say when he came to bring his rent on May 1st?

To Anna.

Tell these two dreamers. You were there too, tell them.

ANNA

Laplante said it as a joke.

ANTONIO

A joke? We know you, you always stand up for the people. After all the bottles of wine I gave him, after all the tomatoes...

Lifting his head, he shouts.

Ribusciato, morto di fame!

Speaking in his natural voice again.

He dared to call me *Señor Rossi* — even when I told him a hundred times that in Italian you say, *Signor* and not *Señor* like in Spanish. "Señor Rossi, after the referendum *I'll* live downstairs, *I'll* be the landlord!"

Anna, Gino and Nancy burst out laughing.

Sure, laugh, laugh! You too, go ahead and laugh. You're all the same. You're all like Laplante. Is that what you want to do? To be a bunch of good-for-nothings? A bunch of tenants?

Talking to the characters on stage.

He even tried to scare me by saying that he was going to

the communist parade downtown. Communist... He wasn't even born yet, Maurice Laplante, and I was already a Communist. But he hasn't learned that communism is good only for poor countries. Here we need strong people to stand up for what we have.

> *The noise of a sports car is heard, and the lights fade.*

SCENE EIGHT

In low lighting.

ZIO

Balloons, balloons.

He laughs.

Yes, I know... respect for authority. It lasted twenty years. After that, they chased us like sheep from a wheatfield. In Collina, there were close to two thousand people at the beginning of the Fifties. When my old lady and I left fifteen years ago, the Grade One teacher only had one pupil. You could see the children sitting like old men, paralyzed with solitude and boredom. Emigration had taken their friends away to the land of chocolate and of the future. At the feast of the Patron Saint, we could never find four men the same height to carry him in the procession. Like the Church, he always leaned to the right. There were so many empty houses that it looked like the evacuations during the last war. No, it wasn't the poverty that chased us from our land, but the rich, as soon as we became too dangerous for them. We were thrown helpless to the four corners of the world, weakened by our ignorance and isolation. I was uprooted from my home for the second time in sixty years. My old lady and I had to come here to mind our grandchildren. The housekeeping, the cooking and the *bambini* killed her. Since then, I go visit my four children in turn, one month with each. I have become a beggar, I who at my age could have been the king of the hill.

Moved.

I want my old lady and my village back. The young have to break the wall of silence which surrounds us. They must tell the story of our humiliations and our setbacks. They must give us our hills back, so that we may see far — very far. I want my old lady and my village.

SCENE NINE

Lighting for this scene should be dreamlike. Mario is wearing a T-shirt on which is written "Kiss Me, I'm Italian".

MARIO

Jean-Pierre Tremblay was my friend. He only spoke French. When I used to play hockey in the street, I never played on Jean-Pierre's team. We used to play the Wops against the Peasoups. I used to call them that because it insulted them. After that, when I became friends with Jean-Pierre and chose to play on the same team as him, they couldn't call us spaghettis or peasoups anymore, because we were all mixed together. But my old team thought I'd sold out. And I laughed and was glad, because I was playing with my best friend. I learned to speak French with him. The more they called me a sellout, the more goals I scored. After that, me and him picked teams at random, and we had a lot more fun.

NANCY

Excitedly, reliving that time.

I used to be behind the window, and I watched him play. Every time he scored, I would get so excited, I would scream like crazy.

50

MARIO

I wanted so much to go to school with Jean-Pierre, but my parents didn't want me to. They kept telling me I was too young to understand. Christ, we were kept young for a long time!

MARIO, GINO & NANCY

My parents worked with Jean-Pierre's parents, that's how they ended up learning to talk like them.

GINO & MARIO

But I was sent to school with Bobby, Jimmy, Ricky, Candy, all the Italians from around here. When I had to do my homework, my parents would never help me.

MARIO

Christ, they could never understand anything, so my father bought me the *Encyclopedia Britannica* in forty volumes, to help me with my homework. I was seven. Even Nancy never opened it. "English school is for your future," my father used to tell me. Fuck the future, man. I wanna live now, now, okay?

NANCY

"The future is not important for women, you'll go to French school."

MARIO & GINO

I speak Calabrese with my parents, French with my sister and my girlfriend, and English with my buddies.

MARIO

Christ, things were bad in school! My teacher wanted to talk to my parents, but they never had time. They were working all the time, for the goddam house and our future. The closer the houses were to the church, the more expensive they were, for Christ's sake!

MARIO, GINO & NANCY

Is the future when you're too old after you've been too young?

MARIO & GINO

It's the same reason why my mother came home late and tired. When we were very small, she would bring us to the parish nuns every morning.

NANCY

I didn't want that dress with the crinoline, straight from Italy, for my first communion.

MARIO & GINO

And I didn't want my made-to-measure white suit. It cost so much that every time I got a stain on it, my mother would give me a whack to remind it had cost her two weeks' pay.

MARIO, GINO& NANCY

It was the same thing for the ground floor — we weren't allowed to get it dirty. We still live in the basement.

MARIO

Jean-Pierre could never figure out why I always made

him come in through the garage door. Christ, we couldn't move in the fucking house! All we ever did in there was eat, eat, eat!

MARIO, GINO & NANCY

And my parents wouldn't stop arguing over money problems.

MARIO

Christ, I really didn't want to have the same problems they had, so I started working weekends, and after a while I quit school. I'm already making more than my father. The old man, Christ, still works for nothing.

Turning on his heels, excitedly.

Hey, Ricky, Jimmy, Johnny, did you see the beauty?

Calming down again.

She's so fucking nice, she's gorgeous! She's a real beauty. She must be something special, if the old man likes her. Sure, he'd have preferred an Italian, but when he saw her, he couldn't resist her, my mother is happy, too. I promised we'd go out a lot together. It's incredible, it's the first time I feel like that. It's as if I didn't need anyone else anymore. Before I had her, I used to hang around with my buddies in the pool hall all the time. Now I always find things to do. Yesterday morning, in front of the church, everyone was looking at her. I never kept anything for very long, but her — ah, I'll keep her for a long time. I can't live without her no more. If anything ever happened to my Trans-Am... Fuck, I think I've got the most beautiful car on the fucking market.

Out loud.

53

Hey, Ricky! You wanna ride?

> *Lights dim and the roar of the Trans-Am is heard. Mario appears alone. He is seen near the front of the car gleaming in the light of its parking lights.*

MARIO

Get in! Get in! Get off there, Nancy, you too, Gino. Let's go!

> *Gino plays Ricky: they can't be told apart.*

RICKY

Fuck, what a beauty! Where're we going, Mario?

MARIO

Anywhere, Christ! As long as we get out of here.

> *Mario imitates the noise of the car accelerating.*

RICKY

Straight ahead, there's a fucking broad on the corner.

MARIO

Oh, Christ! She's such an ape!

> *Accelerates.*

RICKY

Hey, man! We passed the church.

MARIO

Look behind. Are people looking at the car?

RICKY

There's nobody.

MARIO

I'm gonna turn here.

Accelerates.

RICKY

Put the radio on.

Deafening music is heard.

MARIO

I'm gonna shut the radio off. I wanna hear the engine.

Both of them imitate the car accelerating.

RICKY

Faster, faster! You forgot your lights, you cocksucker!

The headlights aimed at the audience light up at the same time as Mario says.

MARIO

Christ!

RICKY

Faster, faster, somebody is trying to pass us. Cut him off, Mario, cut him off.

The front of the car is quickly turned to one side of the stage.

Beautiful! They're in the bushes.

Pause.

We'll never go back to Chiuso, eh, Mario? Never again, eh, Mario?

SCENE TEN

Antonio is sitting around in front of his house, a sprig of parsley in his mouth. The Candidate's poster is still hanging outside. The band is heard in the distance. A few moments later, Zio says out loud, Red ones, green ones, white ones, for big and small.

ANTONIO

To Anna, who is already offstage.

I'll be going in a few minutes, Anna.

Ironically.

Tell Gino the second spectator will be late.

He laughs.

Don't let me see Nancy mixed up in this.

ZIO

Far from Antonio, but onstage.

Balloons, balloons.

Even though he already has quite a few, Zio keeps blowing them up.

ANTONIO

Aside.

The mayor of Montreal is right in wanting to hide the poverty. It's ugly, embarrassing, and makes the rest of us who've succeeded in life ashamed.

To Zio, taking out a dollar bill.

How much do you want for all those balloons?

Takes a step toward him, holding out the money. A balloon explodes at the same time.

How much do you want, Zio?

Antonio takes another step and another balloon bursts. Zio picks up the burst balloons — which he was holding — and shows them to Antonio.

ZIO

You see, you're like the priests — you make my balloons burst.

Antonio lifts a foot, and Zio stares at him with a cry of No!

ANTONIO

You make us ashamed with your bicycle and your sharpening wheel during the week, and your balloons on holidays. People like you turn us into a laughing stock.

Several balloons burst.

Why do the balloons break, if I'm not even moving?

ZIO

It's their way of laughing.

ANTONIO

Excited, in the other direction.

It's a shame, a real shame. Even on St. Anthony's Day.

ZIO

St. Anthony's Day is Chiuso's biggest holiday. You can't confuse St. Anthony with anyone else. After John XXIII, he's the great miracle worker. And there's no one with a better head than him. He specializes in real estate. Last year, on his anniversary, we brought him on the candidate's property, close to the pond, where he had just dug. Monsignore and all the priests were there. Two hundred lots sold in one afternoon. Pope John wouldn't have done better!

> *Joining his hands and raising his eyes to heaven.*

St. Anthony, land agent, pray for us!

Pause.

Balloons, balloons.

SCENE ELEVEN

Three buckets, each containing a rag and a little water. Three people are standing in front of the buckets facing the audience, their arms outstretched towards the buckets. A few feet away, a moderator stands before the mike. A large box on whose sides is depicted the Quebec flag is placed on the stage. Booing is heard. The following sentence is repeated out loud: We want the wrestling... *The rags could be little flags.*

THE MODERATOR

Quiet please, yes, yes, you'll get the fight as soon as the priest is through with blessing the wrestlers. But before the wrestling match, we will present a brief play.

Booing is heard.

Quiet please. *Carissimi amici*, here we are again. This year, the thirtieth edition of our multicultural competition requires ability, rapidity, agility, tenacity and an uncommon knack for tidying away on the part of each competitor.

Pointing to the box.

Our surprise award will go to whoever will finish washing his three square meters first. And now, the questions... The first one I have for you is the following: Will the outgoing champion keep his title? The competition should start without delay. The buckets are already in place. We can already see the hands of the three cultural communities appear.

The hands appear.

Keeping time and resorting to an intricate but subtle gestual pattern typical of their distinct cultures, however parallel to each other, towards the purest vintage Quebec water in order to fetch the rags made in one of our own factories with pure virgin cotton by our own Portugese, Greek and Italian workers. Now, lo and behold! Here is the Portugese hand, proudly exposing its rag, immediately followed by the Hellenic hand. Notice how the fado and the sirtaki have molded the specific curve of each hand. Do the fado and the sirtaki make better prerequisites than the tarantella in view of the present competition? That's the second question.

However, it seems that the Italian hand has stiffened up a little, having spent a little too much time in the textile industry! For the time being, Shish-Kebab and fish seem to be critical in the flexibility and strengthening of the muscles implicated here today.

Miracolo! The third rag is coming out of the bucket. Finally, the three are on the race track I see the situation is getting out of hand. Portugal remains in first position. Our champion for the past ten years, Portugal has namely won the first prize for working under the table as well as for the lowest wages two of the prizes keenly sought by the participating cultural communities. Another feather in Portugal's cap? There's something to think about! The competitors are making good progress. They are scrubbing relentlessly, keeping good time. At that rate, it would take less than one hour to clean up the whole subway. Each one goes at it with personal style and passion endowing the space assigned with a clean new look, much like his personality. From now on, ladies and gentlemen, this space will be known as the Crossroad of Culture.

Not convinced, eh? See how the Italian, on all fours, with his face turned left, reminds us of the *lupa di Roma* suckling Romulus and Remo? Are we witnessing the rise of a new culture here, on this floor? A more down-to-earth culture perhaps? Portugal is giving up. Her standard-bearer is showing us the cause of her defeat. One had to expect it! Like always, one of our cultural minorities owes its failure to an Anglo-American multinational. After having scrubbed with the utmost energy, Portugal had to abandon the game because of the sheer presence of this company who is liable to stick around only as Chicklets can! Italy and Greece are still in the game. Greece seems out of breath, whereas Italy is only one rag from victory. This great civilization which gave the whole world something that no other nation had to offer and never will, that is the Italian language, is crossing the finishing line this very instant.

> *He shouts, two or three times.*

Italia, numero uno.

> *The crowd is heard repeating the same thing. The moderator goes and gets the prize — the box. The winner opens it.*

MODERATOR

It's empty!

THE WINNER

It's empty!

SCENE TWELVE

In a park close to the church, Nancy is sitting on a bench.

NANCY

The virgin of Chiuso is packing her bags tonight.

GINO

Excited, after a moment's thought.

You're giving me an idea for the next show. On the stage, we'll put fifty suitcases, no, a hundred, and we'll hand them out to all the women who come to see the show. We won't say a word, like today.

NANCY

You'll do it without me.

GINO

Without you?

NANCY

Yes, without me. I've had enough of being hassled, finding myself in empty theaters or in front of a crowd that's come to see a wrestling match.

GINO

So why are you leaving your family? I thought...

NANCY

It's not my parents, I'm leaving. It's Chiuso.

GINO

You can't do that. After all the work we did, it's ridiculous! There are young people counting on us, women counting on you to speak for them.

NANCY

I'm freeing myself from Chiuso. To be able to speak up better for freedom. I feel like... I have the feeling we're going around in circles. That we've been stuck in the same rut for the past two years. I feel exactly like I do on stage, screaming my revolt, without being able to get out of the box I'm in. Today I feel like all the women from Chiuso, set free a few days a year from their kitchens and factories so they can put on a nice show with the kids for the procession. A show none of them ever enjoys, all lined up holding their *bambino*'s hand, all starched, and proudly parading under the searching gaze of their men standing on the sidewalk in a choreography signed by the priest. What did that vulture say today? "My children, you really went too far. We won't be able to trust you anymore." We get crushed on all sides, I've had enough.

GINO

Yes, go ahead and make knots too. Don't let yourself be crushed.

NANCY

Knots?

GINO

Yes, *macramé*.

NANCY

Gino, I teach teenagers who all have Italian names and who have one culture, that of silence. Silence about the peasant origin of their parents. Silence about the manipulation they're victims of. Silence about the country they live in. Silence about the reasons for their silence. Two-thirds of them hardly finish high school and end up with their parents in the same factories. Those youngsters never come to our meetings or our activities. We have to get to them in the classroom.

GINO

We only need a few, we have to push them to do what we are doing for the parents.

NANCY

We can't do anything for the parents. We have to take care of the young people. We have to find the ways the ghetto-keepers haven't used yet. We must replace the culture of silence by immigrant culture, so that the peasant in us stands up, so that the immigrant in us remembers, and so that the Québécois in us can start to live. Write; fine, but in a way that everyone can understand you. Young people must find themselves in texts written by someone who lived like them, who understands and wants to help them. Their being different has to become a reason for them to struggle, and not a cause of complexes and passivity.

GINO

You're really naive, Nancy. If there's no place for us in Chiuso, how do you expect us to find one in a place where people have been gazing at their navels for the past twenty years. They even refused to let us go to their schools back in the Fifties.

NANCY

That's an old story...

GINO

We're a minority, and a minority which is beginning to speak up is not well regarded. It becomes dangerous, subversive. The only choice we were given was to unite what we are with what they are, the better to squash us under the weight of their majority. I don't feel like writing a play on the subject of *I Live in Shit, and I'm Staying There*, and see critics and academics short of publications pontificating on fate or other such revolutionary themes.

NANCY

You can write what you want, but only if you write in the language of the country will our culture get a chance to affirm itself and become part of theirs. It's now or never.

GINO

Ironical.

Sure, let's hurry up. People have never talked about us so much. But the problem is that the more you talk about immigration, the less you talk about immigrants. After having been job-stealers, strangers, Wops, mafiosi, spaghetti, the others and the ethnics, now we're the allophones. Have you ever heard an uglier term? That should be the registered trade mark of some phone! Take advantage of the fashion, Nancy. Get out of Chiuso, and find yourself a real true-blue Québécois.

NANCY

That's your privilege, and you know it. All your friends married Quebec girls, and you'll probably do the same. Girls like me, if they stay in Chiuso, are condemmed to marry members of the Sons of Italy, liberal militants and English-speaking. For you and your friends, girls like me are not exciting enough. Not flamboyant enough, not sexy enough. We don't carry integration in our dowry chest, we the well-educated virgins of Chiuso. And you want me to stay here? Unlike you, Gino, I'm twice an immigrant over here: as an Italian in Quebec, and as a woman in Chiuso. Stay, Gino, you're a man.

> *Suddenly we hear:* Balloons, balloons, balloons. Fly away with red ones, green ones, white ones. *Zio appears. The three play with the balloons a few moments. Then the lighting changes.*

ZIO

To Nancy.

Come. Come. Fly away with me. I will show you the voiceless people. I will show you the youngsters of Chiuso, its men and women. We will break the silence, and cross Chiuso's walls so as to join forces with the people who are like us. Fly away with me, Annunziata. Annunziata.

SCENE THIRTEEN

In the big room in the basement, Antonio is near the fireplace, which looks like an altar, all in marble. Anna is seated near Nancy. The tension is evident. Suddenly, the roar of Mario's car is heard. It lasts a few seconds. He's not even in the house yet, when he yells, What's for dinner? *We see him appear wearing the same T-shirt, with "Kiss Me, I'm Italian" on it. He repeats,* What's for dinner?

ANTONIO

Turns abruptly.

This isn't a restaurant.

MARIO

I know it's not a restaurant. We always eat the same thing.

ANTONIO

I want the keys.

MARIO

What keys?

ANTONIO

The car keys. I paid for that damn car.

MARIO

Laughs.

But you're gonna have to hire a chauffeur.

ANTONIO

I'll learn. The keys — right now.

MARIO

To Nancy.

What did you do to the old man, for Christ's sake? You can't talk to him!

To Antonio.

If I'd known, I wouldn't have come home. Take the goddam keys! I don't need your car, for Christ's sake. Three of my buddies have cars.

ANTONIO

Not only that. Get your weights out of the garage. I need the place for the car.

MARIO

Fuck, I'm going to move out of here. I don't need your fucking car, Man. I don't need your fucking garage, Man. Go and live in there, that's the only place where peasants feel at ease.

Mario exits. Anna takes a few steps in his direction, but is stopped by a screaming Antonio. Anna sits down crying.

ANTONIO

Approaches Nancy.

Is that why we sent you to school for sixteen years? To put us down in public? Is that what you teach your students: to make fun of their parents? Look for a husband instead of wasting your time putting on plays.

NANCY

I'm definitely not going to repeat my mother's mistake.

ANNA

Admonishing her daughter.

Nancy!

ANTONIO

To Nancy.

You think your mother made a mistake?

ANNA

The mistake started two years after we got married, when you left to come here, Antonio.

Pause.

I was young, too. You left me alone for four years biting my pillow. My rage, Antonio, turned little by little into indifference. All the time you left me under the supervision of Collina and your father. For months and months I tried to quench the fire in me with rosaries, masses and black dresses. Four years was too long, both for me and Annunziata. You became a stranger, and you stayed a stranger.

ANTONIO

So why did you come here?

ANNA

Because there's only one thing worse that being a woman in Chiuso: being an emigrant's work-widow in Collina. Four years, Antonio, that's a long time.

ANTONIO

I couldn't let you come sooner.

ANNA

You got used to city women's perfume pretty quick. On me, you could smell the sweat and the earth from Collina. I could wait, I disgusted you.

ANTONIO

We had Mario here. It's not the holy ghost who made him.

ANNA

We made him like all the rest, without looking at each other and in the middle of a pile of clothes. Remember, you called the Jew two weeks after I got here. He didn't waste any time. He came with his sewing machine, his rags, and his alms.

ANTONIO

It's not home here, at first it's always hard for everyone.

ANNA

It's a beginning that's lasted for twenty years.

ANTONIO

Go back to Collina, now that my parents are dead. There is no one left to watch you. You won't even be a an emigrant's work-widow. *I'll* be the emigrant's work-widower.

ANNA

You don't emigrate twice. Collina has changed, but we stayed just like we were twenty years ago. Except that if we'd stayed in the village we would have changed like everyone else, we would be like everyone. But here we're even different from our tenants upstairs.

ANTONIO

Especially them. I don't want to have anything to do with those good-for-nothings.

NANCY

Even with Jean-Claude, who comes to pick you up every morning in his car to take you to the factory?

ANTONIO

Him, he's not a Québécois like the others.

NANCY

Even your sister-in-law Jeannette?

ANTONIO

She's not a Québécois like the others, either.

NANCY

Even with Paul Tremblay, who you go hunting with every autumn?

ANTONIO

But it's not the same with him. He's a friend. He's not a Québécois like the others.

NANCY

What about Pierre, Jacques, René and the rest of your co-workers?

ANTONIO

Jacques and René aren't Québécois — both of them come from the Gaspé.

NANCY

Picking up a local Italian paper.

Continue reading your Italian paper and watching your Italian program on TV. For a whole generation now, they've been reinforcing old prejudices and telling the same old stories.

ANTONIO

There are things...

NANCY

...that I can't understand because I'm too young...

ANNA

... and others that I can't understand because I'm a woman.

NANCY

You're the only one to understand everything because you're neither young nor a woman.

ANTONIO

I know that I had go through hell when I got here. I didn't find an apartment with everything in it like you did. I found no one here except bosses who kept telling me to do more, and *Francesi* who scorned me.

To Nancy.

You who are interested in Blacks, don't forget that we Italians were the Haitians of the Fifties. But you, you're not a real immigrant, you can't understand that.

NANCY

I'm the daughter of real immigrants, and that's quite enough. My life has not been much better that yours, and Mario's will be ten times worse.

ANTONIO

Mario is young. He's got his whole life in front of him. It's not the end of the world if he works in my factory. He's getting a chance to see how hard I worked.

ANNA

That's it. That's America for you. It's a big factory, where each worker brought his son, like you, to see for himself all the sacrifices they made. *Santa Maria!* When are we going to break the goddamn chain? Why is it always the same ones who work in the factories? Some of the things we did, Antonio, were not right. We wasted our lives paying for a house that's too big and too expensive for us.

ANTONIO

We have a big house all to ourselves, almost all paid up, and it's in the best neighbourhood in Montreal.

Nancy laughs very loudly.

It's new, and real clean.

ANNA

We worked too hard for nothing. We could have kept the old house, which we would have finished paying for a long time ago. Maybe we could have taken vacations with the kids, paid more attention to them...

ANTONIO

We did everything we could. We did like everyone else.

ANNA

Like everyone else... What I care about is what *I* did. In all my life, Antonio, I'll never had the joy of welcoming my children after school with a snack. I was a prisoner in the factory with forty other mothers like me. At lunch, we fought over the phone telling our kids who came home from school what to eat, and especially to remind them that we were preparing their futures on our sewing machines... Mario's future is a loser's future.

75

ANTONIO

Mario is not a loser!

NANCY

He didn't even finish tenth grade.

ANTONIO

That doesn't mean a thing.

ANNA

Look at me. When I'm not working to pay off this house, I'm working at cleaning it. We don't even allow ourselves to live in it. We live in the basement like moles, because we made a museum out of the ground floor.

ANTONIO

You wanted the French Provincial, velvet and fixtures down to the floor, for Christ's sake!

ANNA

Because in Chiuso you can't live otherwise, without looking like the lowest of the low. But I don't want any more velvet or crystal or fancy living room.

> *With a sudden gesture, she knocks a curio off the table, then bursts into tears.*

I'm afraid, Antonio, I'm afraid of only living just long enough to finish paying off the house, like Christina, like Rosa or like Antonietta.

ANTONIO

We're not poor like we were before.

NANCY

Stop thinking you're rich because you own a house. The only thing Mama did for the past twenty years was supervise the poverty, this white brick crypt where the only time there's life is when there's an argument, and the only brave deeds are your sacrifices. Since you got married, you keep blaming Mama for the lack of money. Will you ever understand that they succeeded in making you feel guilty in order to keep you from forcing your bosses to raise your starvation wages.

ANTONIO

It's not what we earn that counts, but what we put aside. Besides that, I haven't been to college like you. I don't even have a real job.

NANCY

As long as you think it's because of your lack of education that you deserve the wages you're getting, you'll never have the courage to ask for your due.

ANTONIO

I think I'm lucky to be working, things being what they are. Since the separatists came to power, there's no more work. Each morning, there are at least five people lined up in front of the factory door looking for a job. It's no use asking for a raise, I'd be fired before long.

NANCY

You're always scared of something.

77

ANTONIO

Yes, I was scared. Scared to be deported when I got here. Scared of losing my job and my home. I was also afraid of seeing you out on the street.

NANCY

That's the fear we have to bring out in public, to get rid of it together, so that it doesn't get the better of you individually.

ANTONIO

We must start by remaining united at home if we don't want to be afraid any more.

NANCY

And continue tearing ourselves apart between four walls, while Mario and me close windows and doors so that the neighbours don't hear us. I'm stifling here. This house is the symbol of your slavery and the deprivations imposed on Mario and me. It's a diabolical lure that kept you tied to your work for twenty years, it turned you into workers as obedient and docile as sheep.

ANTONIO

Sheep?

To Anna, beside himself.

Did you hear? "Sheep!"

Then to Nancy.

It's for you and Mario that we did all this.

NANCY

For me? For Mario? He doesn't even want your car anymore. Say instead that you were made to sacrifice your lives on the altar of your progeny, while letting people like your candidate get fat on your work. What do you want us children to do with a house built on the exploitation of our parents? It symbolizes injustice.

ANTONIO

Exploitation? Injustice? You don't want this house anymore? Leave. I need this house. I'll always need it! Because I'm a real immigrant, and for people like me, the house is more than just a house... much more than a house. It's... It's...

> *The lighting intensifies on Antonio, who is transfigured and looks as though in a trance.*

An immigrant worker is less than a worker. An immigrant father is less than a father. An immigrant husband is less than a husband. My house had to be big to contain all my dreams. It had to be beautiful like Anna on our wedding day. It had to be warm like Nancy when she was still Annunziata. For an immigrant, a house is more than a house. Here, I don't have any wheat fields to stroke. Here, I have no ancestor to protect me. Here, I have no hills to breathe on. For an immigrant, a house is more than a house. When you feel the earth tremble under your feet, when anxiety never stops suffocating you, when your country and your family have abandoned you, then the house is much more than a house. The house is a bit like my country. At today's celebration, with the band, the singing, the village which I hadn't seen for several months, I felt at home. I didn't feel like a stranger any more. It's always like that when Chiuso is celebrating: when the church bells ring, I open windows and doors to let the music in, the singing and the friends from the village, to drink wine and play *morra* like in Collina. Collina! Collina! Collina!

ZIO

Repeats part of the initial monologue to recreate the atmosphere surrounding the departure.

Balloons... balloons.

Then, in a dreamlike lighting.

"Don't forget to write, Antonio, send pictures, lots of pictures."

Pause.

"You're lucky, Antonio."

Balloons... balloons.

SCENE FOURTEEN

Same room in basement. A suitcase near the door has been added.

ANTONIO

We weren't made to emigrate. We were too ignorant to know what to do here.

NANCY

Understanding.

You're mistaken. They wanted workers like you, shaped by poverty and fascism that kept you ignorant. And you, Mama, ask the Haitians, who are more and more numerous in your factory, how their country is governed.

ANNA

I only know that the Haitians are working at maximum wages.

NANCY

Minimum wages, Mama.

ANNA

For them, it's maximum wages. It seems that in their

country it's like in our country a hundred years ago, and even worse.

ANTONIO

What do they want? They're niggers, after all. They can't compare themselves to us. For centuries, we dominated all of the civilized world, we... (*pause*) ... after civilizing them. We are direct descendants of the Romans.

NANCY

Who were slaves for the most part.

ANTONIO

Beside himself.

Floorwashers and sheep, I suppose?

Aggressive.

What are you still doing here? Your suitcase is ready. What are you waiting for to leave?

Shouts in Italian.

Puttana!

Nancy gets up, but Anna holds her back.

ANNA

You're the one who should leave, Antonio. But you're too well off here.

ANTONIO

I was always too well off. I was too well off when I was a farmer. I was too well off when I was here alone. I was

82

too well off when I carried thirty bricks at a time on my shoulder, ten hours a day, two hours free for the boss.

Shows her his scar.

See my scar? That goes to prove how well off I was. I suppose that's a privilege too?

ANNA

Me, of course, I never did anything. I don't have a scar on my shoulder. My scar, Antonio, is deep in my heart. I feel guilty, me. That's my scar. I feel guilty because Chiuso accuses me. Because Chiuso is a male. Because in Chiuso the losers are the mother's children and not of the father's.

ANTONIO

Mario is young. He's going to change with the years. He speaks three languages, he's healthy, he has a house...

NANCY

Everything by Chiuso's standards. You sent him to school where they teach him the language of your bosses, thinking he would become like them. Mario will learn fast. It's not the language that makes the boss, but the background: his wealth, his power. School has turned Mario into what it turned most of those who have no culture at home. It has discouraged them, so that they can always be the ones to be deprived.

Mockingly.

But of course, he's got his health and the Palazzo Rossi.

ANTONIO

And you, how on earth did you get educated? Are we only responsible for Mario's failure?

NANCY

I was just like Mama. I was a servant for you every time she wasn't there. And if Mario had been older, I'd have had to play servant for him too.

ANTONIO

A servant? Your mother is my wife. Tell her it's not true, Anna. Tell her. Tell her. Tell her.

Anna approaches Zio who holds out the balloons in her direction.

ZIO

Don't cry. Anna. Your Antonio is not going to prison, he's going to America.

Addolorata

For Ginette

THE CHARACTERS

Addolorata	29 years old
Lolita	19 years old
Johnny-Giovanni	19 and 29 years old

Lolita and Addolorata. Two moments in the life of the same person. Lolita is nineteen; Addolorata, twenty-nine. Except for the beauty mark on her cheek, Addolorata has changed a lot. Not only has she aged physically, she has matured. Addolorata wears black stockings, shoes and dress, while Lolita wears a bright, flowered dress.

Johnny-Giovanni, Addolorata's nineteen-year-old fiancé and husband, does not physically change, yet still has much to learn. He is simply dressed. We will notice that after the wedding he does not call himself Johnny anymore but Giovanni.

The set consists of two little tables on both sides of the stage, and two chairs. On each table is a small cardboard box containing letters. There are also a telephone and a telephone book.

The narrator may wear a mask. The music should evoke the folklore of Southern Italy.

PROLOGUE

*Giovanni and Addolorata have been on one
side of the stage for a little while. Giovanni
stands; Addolorata sits. The narrator enters.
At first, the music is scarcely audible.*

NARRATOR

Giovanni and Addolorata immigrated to our building
twenty years ago. In a few moments, you will witness
the sad story of this young couple who live on the thirteenth floor. In this building, the thirteenth floor is the
highest, whereas the fourteenth floor, where the first
tenants still live, is the basement. Greeks, Portuguese,
Spaniards and Haitians live on the other floors. I've
been living on the thirteenth floor for the past fifteen
years. Many came before me, others have yet to come.
In our building, the colour of every floor is different,
and so are the languages we speak. We, for instance,
wear brown clothes. Only the actors will be spared in
this play. For some time lately, we have been forced to
speak the language of the twelfth floor, which, in any
case, we speak more often than the language of the first
floor. It is here, in the theatre, that landlords and building supervisors learn about the kind of life we lead.
They come down from their sunny floors once a week,
usually Saturday night, and as you would expect, are
convinced that Giovanni and Addolorata are the only

ones to blame for their own condition, and furthermore should not complain, since in many other buildings, people don't even have anything to eat.

Lighting changes. Music becomes louder.

There are thousands of Addoloratas. But don't look for them where the sun rises. They are the ones whose smiles have waned. They are the ones who live in the dark. Always look for them on the thirteenth floor, in the crowd at a factory exit. Look for them among those with swollen legs, broken backs, ravaged souls and aged faces. They are there, at the corner of St. Lawrence and Chabanel, or on St. Urbain and Port-Royal. If one of them should fall, help her. She may be my sister, my mother or your own. The sunny floors are off-limits to them. They find consolation, however, in the fact that the basement dwellers had their building confiscated, and in the fact that those twelfth-floor residents who believe they own the building, are merely its custodians. There are thousands like Giovanni, as well. But don't look for them where the sun rises. They are the ones whose smiles have waned. They are the ones who live in the dark. Look for them on the thirteenth floor, among the rootless ones, the marginal ones, among those who always crash against closed doors. They are there, in St. Michel or St. Leonard, workers or the unemployed, in factories or poolrooms. If one of them should fall, help him up. He may be my brother. And if he gets back on his feet, walk with him because he's probably your brother too.

The music continues for a while. Then dark-ness.

SCENE ONE

Lighting on Lolita. Lolita is on her knees washing the floor. Near her is a pail of water which she moves from time to time. On the floor, a can of Ajax lies overturned. After a few seconds, Johnny enters.

JOHNNY

Abruptly.

I wanted to come yesterday, but I couldn't. I argued with my old man till midnight. He wanted us to invite our boss. Christ! Tell me about it: having my boss on my back even on my wedding day!

He hands her some sheets of paper.

Those are the guests on our side. About two hundred.

LOLITA

Put them on the table.

She goes on with her work.

JOHNNY

Christ, you could stop a minute. You're not at the factory here.

LOLITA

My mother went into the hospital yesterday. There's no
one left but me to do the housework.

JOHNNY

Don't panic. You've got the whole afternoon to do that.
Come for a ride in my car. I'm on my lunch break.

LOLITA

I can't.

JOHNNY

You're missing something.

> *He pretends he is pressing on the horn and
> imitates the sound.*

Ta ta ta ta ta ta.

> *Lolita lifts her head, manages a little smile.
> Giovanni is exuberant.*

Yes, I had a musical horn put in. Ta ta ta ta ta ta. Ya
coming?

LOLITA

I can't, Johnny. Did you see the list on the table?

JOHNNY

What list?

LOLITA

The list of all the things I have to do.

JOHNNY

You could finish that tomorrow if you don't have time to get through it tonight.

LOLITA

You don't know my father.

JOHNNY

I'm practically your husband. I'm going to tell your father that from now on he's not the only one who can tell you what to do.

LOLITA

I'm not doing it for him. It's for my mother.

JOHNNY

Wipes his feet.

Okay. I get the message. I'm going.

Pause.

What's this white powder? It's all over the floor.

LOLITA

That's Ajax. My father does that every morning before leaving. To make sure the whole floor gets washed.

JOHNNY

Christ!

LOLITA

His boss does the same thing to him at the factory.

Johnny remains standing with his back to the audience. The lighting changes. After few seconds, Addolorata appears, dressed in black. She does not say a word. She gets on her knees and Lolita hands her the brush. Lolita rises, and exits. Addolorata starts to wash the floor while Giovanni sprinkles the cleaner.

SCENE TWO

The stage is completely lit. Everything is as before, except the pail of water is gone. The two women are on the phone.

ADDOLORATA

Last night? We ate roasted lamb head. We didn't eat here.

ADDOLORATA AND LOLITA

Tonight?

ADDOLORATA

Tonight, we're having cavatelli.

LOLITA

Polenta and sausages.

ADDOLORATA AND LOLITA

Tomorrow? I really don't know what we're having tomorrow. I really don't know.

A door slams. Both women jump.

ADDOLORATA AND LOLITA

I can't talk to you anymore. He just came in. You'll tell me about it the next time.

They hang up, both very upset. Then, in a quavering voice:

LOLITA

Is that you, Papa?

ADDOLORATA

Is that you, Giovanni?

Pause. Addolorata sits down.

ADDOLORATA AND LOLITA

It must be the wind.

Forcing a big smile.

I don't know what got into me to have been afraid of the wind.

Each one empties a box on a table and out come dozens of envelopes.

LOLITA

Excited, she gathers the envelopes in her hands and then drops them on the table.

All those people at my wedding? If everyone comes, there will be almost four hundred guests. It's going to be the biggest and the most beautiful wedding!

She makes small, even piles.

ADDOLORATA

Not many people came to see you, Mamma. It's always the same thing at funeral parlors. They come to be seen themselves. They come to meet people from the *villaggio* they haven't seen for years to talk about their houses and children. They all have the most beautiful house and the most beautiful children. The children are all at the top of their class and are all going to be doctors or lawyers. Only my children... And aside from all of that, we have to thank them for coming, we have to send them a picture of you, Mamma, that they'll throw in the garbage. We even have to thank them...

LOLITA

She opens the envelopes and reads in a solemn tone.

"You are cordially invited to attend the wedding of Miss Addolorata Zanni and Mr. Giovanni Manzo on the fourteenth of July, 1971 at Our Lady of Pompei Church. The ceremony will take place at 1 p.m. with a reception to follow at 7 p.m."

Very excited.

Five hours to take the pictures. My album will be as thick as the phone book. I'm really lucky.

Worried.

I only hope it won't rain.

ADDOLORATA

She opens the envelope and reads.

"Our most sincere thanks for your condolences at the passing of Mrs. Gloria Zanni, the seventeenth of June, 1981. Her daughter, Addolorata Manzo."

LOLITA AND ADDOLORATA

Lolita: excited; Addolorata, serious.

Mr. Giacomo Pirro.

They look for his address in the telephone book.

LOLITA

Mr. Giacomo Pirro. 7527 Fabre St., Montreal.

ADDOLORATA

Mr. Giacomo Pirro, 428 St. Leonard de Vinci St...

Corrects herself.

... Léonard de Vinci St., St. Leonard.

LOLITA

Antonio Gambino, 742 de Gaspé St., Montreal.

ADDOLORATA

Antonio Gambino, 912 Rome St., St. Leonard.

LOLITA AND ADDOLORATA

Pasquale Stabile, 5240 St. Urbain St., Montreal.

LOLITA

Carlo Bottega, 3725 Jean-Talon St. East, Montreal.

ADDOLORATA

Carlo Bottega, 526 St. John XXIII St., Ville d'Anjou.

LOLITA

Rocco Spada, 2342 des Carrières St., St. Leonard.

ADDOLORATA

Rocco Spada, 246, Des Ormes Blvd., Nouveau-Bordeaux.

LOLITA

Adriano Campo, 7943 Garnier St., Montreal.

ADDOLORATA

Adriano Campo, 6782, de la Consitution Blvd., Rivière-des-Prairies.

LOLITA

It will be two months from now, I will be able to do what I want. I won't have you on my back anymore, Papa. Never again.

ADDOLORATA

Now that you're gone, Mamma, now that you're not there anymore, I can't make you sad. One thing is sure, I won't have you on my back anymore, Giovanni. Never again.

LOLITA AND ADDOLORATA

At last, I will be able to do what I want.

Addolorata and Lolita get up abruptly.

ADDOLORATA

Oh! My tomato sauce is burning!

SCENE THREE

Lolita returns from the kitchen. Normal lighting.

LOLITA

I've got it all over me. I got there just before the sauce started to stick to the bottom. Thank goodness!

Stops stirring.

There's something I don't understand. Why is it that when water boils, it doesn't splash all over the place, but when tomato sauce boils and you take off the lid, it's like fireworks. You get it everywhere. Everywhere.

She starts stirring the sauce again.

I even almost got it some in my eye. Lucky I closed my eyes in time.

She takes a spoonful of sauce.

I've been doing this ever since I was nine.

Blows on it. Tastes it.

Tuesday and Thursday. Sunday, it's my mother's turn. At home, after the language issue, the sauce is the cause of most arguments. It can't be too sour, or too sweet, or too brown, or too red, or too spicy, or too salty, or too thick, or too runny. It's so important that they repeat it every Sunday on the Italian television news broadcast. They should do the same thing on the CBC news instead of always talking about politics or catastrophies. For example, last Sunday, after a news coverage of the last earthquake, Mr. Pagliacci himself told us how to make a good sauce with tomatoes he imports from Italy. He really puts himself out for us. I think the program is really good. We can't just stop eating because some people are starving and freezing to death. It's already bad enough to see them die on television. After all, they only have to emigrate like everybody else. I don't know why people insist on staying in Southern Italy. If they like it so much, they can just go there for a holiday. I like Mr. Pagliacci's program for another reason. It allows me to practice real Italian. The Italian the rich people speak.

Pause.

No, that's not it... I have a rich uncle, but he doesn't speak that kind of Italian.

She stops to think.

I don't know the people who speak that Italian...

Pause.

... and the Italian of travelogs... I'm going to learn lots of languages and go everywhere. I'm going to travel around the world.

Pause.

But first... but first, I would like to go downtown at least once and dance in a real discotheque.

SCENE FOUR

Johnny appears by Lolita's side. Johnny looks worried. She is surprised to see him at this hour.

LOLITA

What are you doing here? You're not working?

Johnny doesn't answer; he is motionless.

You shouldn't have come. Don't you know my father yet?

JOHNNY

Fuck your old man.

LOLITA

Johnny...

JOHNNY

I don't give a damn about your father, if you really want to know.

LOLITA

Johnny, how can you talk like that?

JOHNNY

How do you want me to talk? I just lost my job.

LOLITA

What? Again?

JOHNNY

Yeah. For the third time this year.

LOLITA

Why?

JOHNNY

How I am supposed to know? Do you think the boss explains anything? He just told me that there was no more work.

LOLITA

That's an explanation.

JOHNNY

Fuck, we worked overtime until last week because there was too much work. Now they tell us there's no more.

LOLITA

If that's the case, they'll call you back soon for sure. The Bay always calls me back. They've called me back five times this year.

JOHNNY

But me, fuck, they won't call me back.

LOLITA

You're really...

She is looking for the word.

You're not an optimist.

JOHNNY

What?

LOLITA

Everything looks black to you.

JOHNNY

I tell you they're not going to call me back. They're closing their goddamn factory.

LOLITA

They won't be able to keep it closed all the time. They'll reopen it, you'll see.

JOHNNY

They are not going to reopen it because they're leaving. They're getting out of here.

LOLITA

Where are they going to go?

JOHNNY

South America. At least if...

Lolita interrupts him.

LOLITA

South America? I've got a cousin there.

JOHNNY

He looks at her, surprised.

You look happy!

LOLITA

I just told you I have a cousin over there. But why are they moving so far away?

She quickly answers her own question.

Maybe it's because it's a lot warmer. My cousin sent me a picture of herself on the beach on Christmas day. She was going swimming.

JOHNNY

Those companies would move to the North Pole if there was a buck to be made there.

LOLITA

She thinks.

Maybe the boss is South American.

JOHNNY

How should I know? We never even saw him. Seems he has so many factories, he doesn't have time to visit them all.

LOLITA

That's not serious. Let them move. It's like it is here in July, you'll see a lot of houses empty out, but in the end

they fill up again. Last year, our tenant moved to Roxboro, and you know who took his place?

Pause.

Say something...

JOHNNY

Do you think I care?

LOLITA

A family from Roxboro, Johnny. Would you believe it?
So what if your factory moves to South America? I'll
bet you a South American factory is going to move here.

Pause. Johnny shrugs his shoulders.

Besides, there's work everywhere.

JOHNNY

Porcocane, you're blind.

LOLITA

Don't be angry with me. I'm only trying to help.

JOHNNY

I'm not angry. What makes you think I'm angry?

LOLITA

Yes, you're angry. Every time you speak Italian, it
means you're angry.

JOHNNY

Furious.

You're telling me there's work everywhere. Fuck, half of my friends can't find a job. Jimmy can't even drive his car because he can't afford the insurance.

LOLITA

I'll pay your insurance, but you don't speak to me in English anymore.

JOHNNY

Beside himself.

You never understand anything. It's the third job I've lost this year.

Mocking.

"Come work with me," that's what my father used to say. "Sure, it doesn't pay much, but it's a steady job, it's a big company. I've been working there for the past seventeen years. Never lost a day." That's what he said, my old man. So I went. And two months later, I was out of a job. I wasn't even there for seventeen weeks.

LOLITA

Your father too?

JOHNNY

The factory closed. Not only for me. It closed for everybody, dummy.

LOLITA

Impatient.

You'll tell me the rest on the phone, Johnny. You've got to go. My father can't find us together.

JOHNNY

I can't go back home right away. The old man is going to kill me.

LOLITA

What have you done that's so bad?

JOHNNY

If you had only seen him when I quit the factory. As far as he's concerned, I'm lazy. The boss shut the factory, but I'm the one to blame. He wanted me to stay on for another month.

LOLITA

You just told me that the factory is closed.

JOHNNY

There's still a month's work packing up the machines.

LOLITA

And you didn't stay?

JOHNNY

You're like my father. Stay to pack up the machines? Me? I punched and I left right away! They'll never make me dig my own grave. Only the old men stayed. Those people would dig their own graves if they were paid to... Christ, it's not the machines I would have packed but the bosses... Besides, I wanted to set fire to the dump, to blow it up. But with all the old guys there...

Pause.

108

It's because of the old guys that the plants close down. I've never been to South America, but I'm sure there must be a gang of old people there ready to get other people's factories.

LOLITA

Don't say that. My cousin is there.

JOHNNY

Fuck, your cousin too. I don't give a damn.

Pause.

I had a chance to learn something. I was working on a great big machine, big as the kitchen. Me, alone. I pushed the button and it started: *boom, clack, boom, clack, boom, clack.* It folded sheets of stainless steel like paper in less time than it takes to scratch your nose. You had to move fast. I'd remove the piece of folded metal, stack it on my left, take a strip of metal from a pile on my right, and put it in the machine: left, right, machine, left, right, machine...

Faster.

... left, right, machine, left, right, machine.

He wipes his forehead.

I didn't have time to fool around. I wonder if in South America they'll know how to do that: left, right, left, right, left, right.

Pause.

I alone controlled my machine. I had a trade. Finally, I had a trade. That's what a trade is: when you can do something alone... and when you feel like somebody. Christ, I was beginning to feel important.

109

LOLITA

Understanding.

Don't think about that anymore, Johnny. When we're married, we'll find jobs — jobs that pay well too.

Pause.

JOHNNY

It's really strange. When we lived in the *villaggio*, everybody was emigrating to where the big companies were. Now the big companies move to where they can find cheap labour.

LOLITA

Tenderly.

We'll find jobs, Johnny. Jobs that pay well. You'll see.

Suddenly.

Oh, my tomato sauce!

SCENE FIVE

Lighting evokes a dreamlike atmosphere. Only Johnny and Lolita are lit. Addolorata remains in darkness.

JOHNNY

I don't know if we should. I'm afraid.

LOLITA

Afraid of what?

JOHNNY

I'm out of work.

LOLITA

I'll work. Don't be afraid, Johnny.

JOHNNY

Week-ends at The Bay, that's not much. We should wait. Fuck, I'm really afraid. We should wait. The invitations haven't been sent out yet. It's not too late.

LOLITA

She throws her arms around Johnny's neck.

I can't go on living with my father anymore. I can't.

She cries.

Lighting on the three characters. Johnny, otherwise motionless, moves his head in the direction of the speaker, except when both speak at once.

ADDOLORATA

Ten years, that's enough. I can't anymore.

LOLITA

I can't stand being cooped up in the house all the time — even on Saturday night.

JOHNNY

Okay, okay, we'll get married, fuck.

ADDOLORATA

I'm fed up with being alone all the time.

JOHNNY

It's not my fault.

LOLITA AND ADDOLORATA

I've had it.

LOLITA

... to have to see my friends in secret.

JOHNNY

Okay, we'll get married.

ADDOLORATA

... not to have any friends. Not to be able to go out.

JOHNNY

What do you want me to do about it?

LOLITA AND ADDOLORATA

I've had it...

LOLITA

... with his slapping...

ADDOLORATA

... with your rapes...

LOLITA

... with his yelling...

ADDOLORATA

... with the fighting...

LOLITA

... with this house...

ADDOLORATA

... with Jean-Talon Street...

LOLITA

… with being taken for a piece of dirt…

ADDOLORATA

… with being nothing but a piece of dirt.

They look at Johnny.

LOLITA AND ADDOLORATA

With never deciding anything. I've had it.

LOLITA

… with being his daughter…

ADDOLORATA

… with being your wife. Ten years is enough.

JOHNNY

To Lolita.

I understand.

LOLITA AND ADDOLORATA

I want to change life.

JOHNNY

I understand.

LOLITA AND ADDOLORATA

I want to breathe too.

JOHNNY

To Lolita.

All right, shut up, I understand.

He covers his face with his hands.

SCENE SIX

Total darkness. After a few moments, the narrator reappears shining a flash-light and he addresses the public.

NARRATOR

Don't worry. This is only a warning. This happens to us all the time. The first-floor superintendents cut the power when they find the actors' remarks unacceptable. But, fortunately, this only happens once during the show. If they are not satisfied with the rest of the play, they don't cut the power again: they simply ban all further performances. I hope you have no intention of seeing this play again. The first-floor superintendents have already informed us of the type of play they prefer. These are light comedies, psychological dramas, or any other type of play in which fate motivates the action. On the thirteenth floor, that type of drama is considered prostitution.

He moves as if about to leave.

Oh, I forgot. For the last while, they've grown very fond of plays in which woman sees her husband or father as the sole source of her unhappiness. They've never had such a laugh. Moreover, they're getting ready once again to increase interest rates and unemployment.

The power comes back on.

Oh! it's begun.

SCENE SEVEN

*Enter Giovani carrying a pool cue in one hand.
Addolorata continues to write addresses.
Giovanni throws a bank book on the table.
Nobody talks for a while. Giovanni takes
advantage of this time to repair his pool cue.*

ADDOLORATA

What are you up to? Not at your poolroom?

Long silence.

GIOVANNI

Not finished yet? You've been writing these addresses
two whole days now.

ADDOLORATA
Shyly.

There are more than two hundred letters to send out.

GIOVANNI

Two hundred pictures of your mother...
Laughs.

If Italians didn't take so many pictures at weddings,

baptisms and funerals their mortgages would be paid up by now. When I think that ten years ago, it cost us four hundred dollars for the wedding pictures. Imagine what it would cost today!

ADDOLORATA

Casts an ambiguous glance.

We never should have.

GIOVANNI

Repeats mechanically.

Yeah, we never should have done it.

Recovers awareness.

What do you mean by that?

ADDOLORATA

The same thing you mean.

GIOVANNI

Wary for a moment.

It's a waste. Besides, we should never have invited so many people. They didn't even give five dollars a person in gifts.

ADDOLORATA

Still, you were able to buy your poolroom.

GIOVANNI

You forget the house came with it.

Pause.

Tomorrow, we have to make a payment on the house and you still haven't deposited your pay-cheque.

ADDOLORATA

We were supposed to go on a honeymoon with the money from the gifts. Don't you remember?

GIOVANNI

Porcocane. I'm telling you about the cheque you got the day before yesterday, and you're talking to me about something that happened ten years ago.

ADDOLORATA

I remember as if it were yesterday. And I remember each time I give you my cheque. It makes me think about the story my grandfather used to tell me when I didn't want to go to school. "Life," he used to say, "is like a big castle with an infinite number of rooms. Each room has a door, and behind each door there is a key to open the next. You come into the world with the first key — it's not your doing — but the second key is to school." That's what my grandfather used to tell me. Our honeymoon, Giovanni, that was also a key. You threw it into the poolroom and that's why we could never open any of the other doors.

GIOVANNI

I had no work. And besides, I was fed up with being laid off every three months. In the long run, you end up thinking you're useless. You're tossed left and right, like an old rag... At nineteen, it's tough on you. *Anche i coglioni ti tremano.*

ADDOLORATA

You were right, Giovanni. You were right to finance a poolroom for the good-for-nothings around here. It makes you feel better to be surrounded by loafers and maniacs who rub their balls against the sides of the pool table. You should rehire the whore who used to be a waitress the first few years. That would cool them down a bit.

GIOVANNI

You ought to know that educated people come to my poolroom. Educated people who are on our side.

ADDOLORATA

They are so much on our side that you make a real fortune on them. Almost a hundred and fifty bucks a week...

GIOVANNI

... Net. A hundred and fifty bucks a week net, just like you. That's what people like us make. We're not the only ones. Half the Quebecois don't make more.

ADDOLORATA

But not many work until three o'clock in the morning.

GIOVANNI

That's the immigrants' lot. The piece-work you do at the factory is no better. That's the kind of work we've got to take.

ADDOLORATA

You are the one who made me take that job. Nobody else. If I had continued working part-time at The Bay, in time I would have been working a full week. I'd be a saleslady. Behind a clean counter, with clean people, I would wear clean underwear.

GIOVANNI

We needed money. You didn't even make twenty bucks a week-end.

ADDOLORATA

I've been stuck to my sewing machine for the past nine years. I feel like I've rotted away and I'm not even thirty. Not even thirty, Giovanni.

GIOVANNI

If immigration was a good thing, it wouldn't be left to poor people like our parents and ourselves. The same goes for your job. And for my job. Westmount ladies are not going to come down from their castles to work in your place, and their husbands aren't coming to take over my job either. They didn't find the key behind the door, they found it on our backs. Look at them. They aren't the ones who make souvlakis, or drive taxis. They aren't shoemakers or barbers. Who does dangerous jobs, the low-paying jobs? We do. It's always us, the immigrants. It's not working at home that killed your mother. It was her boss at the factory who made her do piece-work. It was always "Faster, faster." She could never work fast enough. We immigrants have one single advantage over the others: when the crunch comes, we don't even see it, we don't even feel it, because we've lived it from the day we were born. But I, Giovanni

Manzo, I'll never let myself be killed by a boss. That's why I work for myself. To look after my own business myself.

ADDOLORATA

You're also going to pay for your poolroom yourself. You won't be getting my pay-cheque anymore.

GIOVANNI

And what am I going to pay the mortgage with? We have to hurry up and pay everything back before it comes due, if we don't want the bank to bleed us for it.

ADDOLORATA

I don't want to have a boss anymore, either.

GIOVANNI

How many times did I tell you to get them to send the work to you at home. You'd be able to look after the kids at the same time, and you'd feel less guilty.

ADDOLORATA

We're not talking about the same thing. My pay-cheque, is the last key I have left. I can't afford to let that one go.

GIOVANNI

Don't bug me with your key stories.

> *He takes the bank book and lays it down on the table.*

And if tomorrow you don't deposit *your* cheque in *my* bank account, I'm sending you back to your father.

He exits.

To my father?

She laughs.

To my father? I won't let go of that key again. I won't let it go anymore.

SCENE EIGHT

The stage is pitch black. We can see nothing but the faces of Giovanni and Addolorata lit by a white light. We hear the sounds of a door squeaking as it was being opened and a key turning in the lock.

ADDOLORATA

I found it. It was behind the door.

GIOVANNI

Where are we, Addolorata?

ADDOLORATA

I don't know, but I see a big room bathed in sunlight with a window on the sea. Look over there: there's a couple in wedding clothes asking us to go and join them.

GIOVANNI

That's not what I see.

ADDOLORATA

They're calling us. Come, Giovanni, come.

GIOVANNI

I don't see the same thing as you.

ADDOLORATA

What do you see?

GIOVANNI

Soldiers. Soldiers everywhere. Hundreds of soldiers running, guns in hand, after a handful of peasants. I recognize my father. He is in front of everyone. Run, Papa, run. Faster. Faster.

Addolorata screams

What's going on? I don't see anything.

ADDOLORATA

Neither do I. How are we going to find the other key? How are we going to find the other doors?

Lighting on Giovanni. A child's voice is heard off-stage.

CHILD'S VOICE

Why did you go so far away to work, Papa? You promised to come home for my first communion. Why didn't you come?

Pause.

I didn't want communion. They forced me to swallow the Host and I spat it out. I told Mamma that I would do my first communion only if you were there. Come back, Papa. Who forced you to go so far away to work? I don't feel like going to school anymore since you left.

Come back, I'm afraid to sleep all alone. Come back fast. I filled a big basket with figs. We'll eat them near the well. There's no water in the well since you left and the sheep have no more lambs. Come back, Papa. I'm afraid to stay alone. I'm afraid. Who forced you to go so far away to work? We need you here. Come back. Come back, Papa. We need you for the *villaggio* fair. There's no one to sing. Come back, Papa.

The music continues for a long while.

SCENE NINE

Addolorata is making her tomato sauce.
Giovanni comes in rubbing his eyes.

GIOVANNI

I can't sleep.

ADDOLORATA

The afternoon isn't meant for sleeping anyway.

GIOVANNI

When do you want me to rest? *Porcocane!*
    Pause.
I don't sleep like I used to since your mother died.

ADDOLORATA

I didn't think you loved her that much.

GIOVANNI

You know I couldn't stand her.

ADDOLORATA

You got rid of her. You should be happy, no?

GIOVANNI

Sure I'm glad she's out of my hair. "Giovanni, you should look for a real man's job. You should keep your wife at home. The children need their mother at home."

Grimaces.

"Working in a poolroom is not a man's job." What's a man's job? Breaking your back at construction work? Being rattled from morning till night by a power jackhammer? Roasting like meat on a grill while laying asphalt? Or maybe it's working in a factory on machines that don't even give you time to breathe? *Porcocane!* What's a man's job?

Pause.

In the evening, when these men come home, everyone is surprised to see them acting like animals. It's hard to do anything else when you're treated like an animal from morning till night. But...

He hesitates, takes a few steps and comes back.

ADDOLORATA

But what?

GIOVANNI

You've changed since she died. You've changed an awful lot.

ADDOLORATA

It must be because I'm happy not to have her in my hair too.

GIOVANNI

But she was always on your side. She always helped you. There's something I don't understand: you've become a real tigress since she died.

ADDOLORATA

Me, a tigress? I just made up my mind to do what I've been wanting to do for a long time.

GIOVANNI

And what is it you've been wanting to do for a long time?

ADDOLORATA

Hesitates.

Leave.

GIOVANNI

Astonished.

What? Where?

Not taking her seriously, mockingly.

You, leave?

ADDOLORATA

Yes, I am going to leave. I don't want to live with you anymore. Do you understand that? That's why I kept my cheque. I can do it now. I would have done it before, but I was afraid my mother would have another heart attack.

GIOVANNI

Still not taking her seriously.

And... when would you have left if...

ADDOLORATA

It's not important, since I couldn't.

GIOVANNI

We've been husband and wife for the past ten years, and all of a sudden...

ADDOLORATA

... for ten years you came in at three in the morning, for ten years we never ate together, for ten years, I lived above your poolroom, listening to your customers' swearing and seeing my children hang around in the back alley. For ten years you haven't cared about the kids, and for ten years I've been handing my cheque over to you. Those are our ten years of marriage: never any pleasure, never any holidays. Since we gave up going to Oka, we don't go anywhere anymore.

GIOVANNI

Oka is an outdoor open sewer. I didn't feel like walking through shit or smelling the smoke of ten thousand barbecues. People like us camp on the side of the highway or squeeze in like sardines at Wildwood. Is that what you want? Go ahead. I'm not interested. Besides, so long as Reagan is in power, the Americans are not going to see my face. They'll never get my money to finance their missiles. You don't understand that. Because of people like you, there are Reagans in power. Will you get it into your head once and for all that we're only immigrants?

131

ADDOLORATA

Exasperated.

Immigrants... We've been here for twenty years now.

GIOVANNI

Forty years from now we'll still be immigrants. *Sempre.* It's not the number of years we stay here that makes immigrants out of us, it's the way we live. In a country where the rich and the employers lead the government around by the nose, poor people and workers are immigrants, even if their names are Tremblay or Smith. If we, the workers, don't make the decisions, we'll never have a country. That's why we're all immigrants. Do you think that those who make the decisions for us think about our interests? Look around you: of all those who came from Italy, one out of a thousand made it at all, and not always honestly either. The most dangerous ones are those who come and drink cappuccino while they keep their little fingers bent.

He mimics the gesture and puckers his lips.

ADDOLORATA

Frankly, you're in good company.

GIOVANNI

If those assholes were my only customers, I would have closed up a long time ago. I told you a hundred times. Some educated people come to my poolroom. And old men. They taught me a lot of things in ten years. Old men are the only books for people like me who aren't used to reading. I learned a lot in ten years.

ADDOLORATA

Except the most important thing. You only talk politics.

GIOVANNI

What's wrong with that? What good is it to kill yourself on the job? Nothing ever changes. Workers' children become workers too, and work their asses off like their parents. Like you, like me. Only with politics can you change anything, and if it doesn't work, we'll blast everything. I'm not the only one to say so. We'll get rid of all the flags. There'll be no more Italian flag, Greek flag or Quebec flag in our way. We won't be divided anymore.

ADDOLORATA

In any case, your politics didn't change much for us, and even less for me.

GIOVANNI

You would have rather had me lock you up in a big house in St. Leonard? That was your mother's dream. You would have had to work two shifts at the factory to pay for your big house, I'm telling you. You'd have had twice as much housework too, especially with all the dust from the Metropolitan and the cement quarries. St. Leonard is like the Olympic Stadium: a big pile of cement that's more than we can afford. Yeah. It's not the stadium we should have covered up, it's St. Leonard.

ADDOLORATA

It's no use. You always talk about the same things.

GIOVANNI

You never understand anything. Go on — make your
mother's dream come true.

With scorn.

Vattene. Non mi rompere più i coglioni.

*Not believing in Addolorata's departure,
Giovanni mocks her.*

You, leave?

Laughs.

You, leave?

Laughs.

SCENE TEN

She takes the guitar and plays a few chords.

LOLITA

I'm learning to play the guitar for Johnny. I'm sure he's going to love that song. It was love at first sight for me anyway.

She sings a verse from "Guantanamera." She plays and sings poorly.

I get shivers all over when I sing that song. I'll sing it to him on our honeymoon. It will keep me busy a bit... and it's so romantic!

She sighs.

When I think I practically missed everything because of my name! With a name like Zanni, you're always last in everything. When I went to CEGEP to register for a Spanish class, there was no room left. I couldn't help it, I burst into tears in front of all the teachers. I won them over! They ended up allowing me to take my Spanish class. I think that was the nicest day of my life, nicer still than my first communion. Anyway, when I went to the first class, it was like going to a party: all my friends were there. All Italians, except for one English girl. Fortunately, she left three weeks later. I never heard anyone pronounce so badly. Those people are really not talented with languages. Maybe that's why they've forced so many people to learn theirs.

Pause.

The Spanish teacher was so... *hermoso y caloroso.* He made us feel at ease right away by singing "Guantanamera." Ever since then, I sing it at least once a day.

She sings a verse.

If it hadn't been for the Spanish course, I wouldn't have stayed in CEGEP long. But even so, one year is enough. There is so much unemployment, it's no use getting an education. Everyone knows that the educated unemployed are much more unhappy than the uneducated unemployed. I don't want to be unhappy. In September, when I register for night school, I'm going to take two Spanish courses. Then I will know four languages. With four languages I can go ahead and get married without being afraid. If Johnny knew four languages, I'm sure he wouldn't be so afraid of getting married.

Silence.

I learned English and French at bilingual school. At French bilingual school. That's why I speak French naturally. I don't even think when I speak. It's the only French bilingual school in Montreal. But the nuns were so strict, we were hardly allowed to do anything. No speaking in the hall. No leaving the school-yard at lunch. No chewing gum. No staying too long in the washroom: one minute to pee, no more. The nun who watched over the washrooms, we used to call her "shit lady".

She laughs.

I'm the one who thought of that name. This is forbidden... that is forbidden... No wander the school was

136

called Notre-Dame-de-la-Défense. In St. Leonard, they already tried setting up English bilingual schools for Italians, but it didn't work out. They realized it was necessary to teach both languages in school because Italians were picking up French in the street. And to pick up French in the street is not worse than learning it in school. It's the same thing for Italian. We don't have to study it: we have it in our blood. For us Italians, school is practically useless. All my friends dropped out as soon as they could. They considered me the brain of the gang. Johnny didn't even finish grade ten. When you're as smart as he is... you always get bored at school. I'm never bored. I'm never bored with my four languages. I can speak English on Monday, French on Tuesday, Italian on Wednesday, Spanish on Thursday, and all four on Friday.

Serious.

On the weekend, I don't talk because my father is home.

Exuberant.

I can also speak English with my friends, French with the neighbours, Italian with the machos, and Spanish with certain customers. With my four languages, I never get bored. With my four languages, I can watch soaps in English, read the French TV Guide, the Italian fotoromanzi, and sing "Guantanamera".

Lighting comes to normal.

When I think that some people get married with only one language and they're happy... I can already picture myself married with four languages. That must be something! But the one I prefer is Spanish. I don't know what I would give to be a real Spanish lady. At The Bay, when I have Spanish customers, I introduce myself as Lolita Gomez. It's so much nicer than Addolorata Zanni. Addolorata is so ugly, that most of my cousins changed their name. The one living in Toronto calls herself Laurie. She's the cousin I like least. She's so weird — she studies things that are for men. She wants to be a "lawyer". She only speaks English. She says she also speaks Italian, but when she tries, she speaks half Italian, half English. I don't know where she's going to go with a language and a half. I have another cousin in Argentina. Her name is Dolores. She's the one who sent me the guitar when my uncle came to visit. Dolores is such a beautiful name. My last cousin is almost as horrible as the one in Toronto. She lives in the *villaggio*. She hasn't changed her name. Still calls herself Addolorata. I can't understand why anyone would call herself Addolorata in 1971. She really talks like a man — always about politics. In the small villages in Italy, there are lots of people like that: a bit backward. When I was on vacation there last year, I didn't go out with her more than twice. I preferred going out with my aunt Rosaria, who took me to see the beautiful sanctuaries. We even went to see Padre Pio. Padre Pio is like Brother André here. That day, he worked so many miracles that I almost wished I were a cripple. I don't mean to say that the crippled weren't crippled anymore after having being blessed by him. No, the blind remained blind and those who were limping kept limping. But they smiled, yes, they smiled. For the first time, they were happy to be crippled. Really happy. That's the miracle. I will never forget that sanctuary. It's not far from my *villaggio*. The weather is always beautiful there. I think it's really the best outdoor place to do these things. Compared to that, politics is so boring. In St. Leonard, we elected two Italian deputies just because they're Italian. I remember they came to our house on the eve of the eletion. They never talked of what they'd do during their term. No. They only talked about wine with my father. After a few glasses, they even sang a few dirty songs with my father.

Laughs shyly.

A real old country scene. They left as soon as they learned my father couldn't vote because he doesn't have Canadian citizenship.

With scorn.

Deputies! Even dogs would have been elected in their place if they could bark in Italian.

Pause, then forcefully.

Even my father could have been elected.

Pause.

My tomato sauce!

SCENE ELEVEN

Addolorata is seated at her table writing addresses.

ADDOLORATA

Thank-you notes is not what I should be sending out... I should write what I think about them. Goddamn family. *Maledetto villaggio!* Big fat Rosa: a real snake. Even at the funeral parlor.

In a mocking tone.

"Still living at the same place, Addolorata? You must like it. My daughter just bought a big house in Rivière-des-Prairies. Your mother was more than a cousin for me. She was a real sister." She even shed a tear, the big hypocrite. It went on and on at the parlor. Everyone shed their approriate tears, and came up with little comments to twist the knife. "You look so much older, Addolorata!" "Your children are so pale, Addolorata!" "Your husband is not at the parlor, Addolorata?" I will no longer have a husband, do you understand?

She reads the names of the women on the envelopes.

I will no longer have a husband. Do you understand, Cristina? Do you understand, Antonietta? Do you understand, Rina? I won't have one anymore. And as for you, I don't want to see you anymore. I'm fed up with seeing you like little frightened puppies next to your wolf-like husbands. I've had enough of your black dresses. I've had enough of seeing your death-like faces next to your husbands who drink and dance at every party. I've had enough of seeing you die for your children. I've had enough of seeing your children all dressed up like fashion plates and being told not to move, not to get dirty. I've had enough of seeing you come out of your basements like moles. I've had enough of seeing you make tons of preserves. Enough of seeing you hide your sicknesses and play the role of the tireless woman. I've had enough of seeing you come back from the factory, prepare supper, serve it, eat standing up, do the dishes, make the sandwiches, sweep the floor, do the laundry, iron, scream at your daughters, go to bed at midnight, get raped by your husbands, get up at six, prepare breakfast, leave before everyone else, run to the factory, stay nailed to your sewing machine, get harassed by your boss, get underpaid, hold your pee, work by the piece, eat at the sewing machine, and start over again and again.

Pause, moved.

I don't want to be like you anymore.

Remains immobilized for a long while, then rises abruptly.

Oh, the tomato sauce.

SCENE TWELVE

Lighting is multicoloured. Very joyous music is heard. Two trophies are to be awarded for the "Queen of the Household" contest. Each contestant holds a trophy in her hand, which is nothing more than a pan mounted on a base of some sort. They also wear masks. The moderator presents the two prize-winners.

MODERATOR

Ladies and gentlemen, here are the two contestants who have tied for first place in the "Queen of the Household" contest.

TWO WOMEN

I won the "Queen of the Household" trophy
Like all queens, I'm very busy.
I reign over my husband and five sons.
And the rest of the day I slave at the factory.

> I'll be queen for a long time.
> This trophy will always be mine.

In the evening, when I get home,
They're all watching television.
I never disturb them, they're so sweet.
When the supper is ready, they come to eat.

142

I'll be queen for a long time.
This trophy will always be mine.

Man has needs he can't control.
In a few seconds, it's all over.
He falls asleep right away.
I know he loves me that way.

I'll be queen for a long time.
This trophy will always be mine.

Since mothers come from Europe and Haiti.
The government saves a lot of money.
Day-care centers are not for me.
I made my old mother come from Italy.

I'll be queen for a long time.
This trophy will always be mine.

Aching back and swollen legs,
Low pay and long working days,
Believe me, I deserved them all.
I'm only an immigrant after all.

I'll be queen for a long time.
This trophy will always be mine

SCENE THIRTEEN

Lolita is wearing a wedding veil over her face. Johnny offers her his arm. The lighting evokes a dreamlike atmosphere.

LOLITA

We won't live like our parents, right, Johnny?

JOHNNY

Fuck, what do you take me for?

LOLITA

Will you be nice to me, Johnny? Will you open the door when we go to a restaurant?

JOHNNY

Hey, fuck, I have manners.

LOLITA

Will you pull out my chair for me?

JOHNNY

Yes, but I won't push it in. I don't like that.

LOLITA

You don't have to, I'll do it myself. Will I also be able to order what I want?

JOHNNY

So long as you eat it.

Laughs. Finds himself funny.

But you'll take an hour to choose.

LOLITA

Excited.

Oh no, I already know what I want.

JOHNNY

What?

LOLITA

I'd like to have escargots.

JOHNNY

What's that?

LOLITA

They taste a lot like garlic.

JOHNNY

Wouldn't be easier just to eat garlic?

LOLITA

Then, we'll hold hands and lean across the table towards each other to talk.

JOHNNY

What will we say to each other?

LOLITA

Well, we could talk about what we're eating.

Organ music is heard.

There aren't many people in church — what a drag.

JOHNNY

You know very well they only come to eat. Don't worry, they'll all show up at the reception tonight.

Organ music stops.

LOLITA

You're going to bring me downtown, aren't you, Johnny?

JOHNNY

What would you like to see?

LOLITA

I only know The Bay.

JOHNNY

Well, that's about all there is to downtown.

LOLITA

What about discotheques?

146

JOHNNY

Discotheques aren't for you.

LOLITA

We could go to the Botanical Garden.

JOHNNY

We're going there for the pictures later on. You'll see, except for the greenhouses, there isn't much. There are a lot more vegetables in your father's garden.

LOLITA

No matter. At least we'll get to go out.

JOHNNY

Lift your veil. We're at the Botanical Garden.

LOLITA

You do it.

Johnny abruptly lifts the veil.

Gently! Gently!

She puts down the veil.

I want to take at least one picture with my veil down.

She poses.

Smile, Johnny. Smile like me.

She lifts the veil. They pose for an imaginary photographer: 1) cheek to cheek; 2) Johnny on his knees; 3) Lolita on her knees; etc. We hear the wedding march played very loudly on the accordion.

We're already at the reception hall! Look at all the people!

JOHNNY

I told you they'd all be there to eat.

LOLITA

You sound like my father, Johnny.

JOHNNY

Hey, there's practically more kids than adults. They've already started running around all over the place. We'll never get any peace.

LOLITA

You sound like my father, Johnny.

JOHNNY

Look at your aunt from Toronto. She's wearing everything she owns. She looks like a Christmas tree. Look at her, wearing three gold bracelets. She can't even lift her arm.

LOLITA

You sound like my father, Johnny. You sound like my father.

JOHNNY

What's wrong with that?

> *Johnny removes her veil. The lighting comes back to normal. Johnny throws himself on her awkwardly. He tries to kiss her.*

LOLITA

She tries to extricate herself.

No, Johnny, my father can come in any minute now.

JOHNNY

Fuck, we'll be married in a couple of months.

He opens her blouse. Tries to kiss her breasts.

LOLITA

Johnny, I hear a noise. My father is coming back. You must go. You must go.

Johnny runs out while Lolita buttons up again.

LOLITA

If my father had seen me.

At the same time, we hear a motor starting up.

Louder, Johnny, louder.

The noise gets louder.

Go on, Johnny.

Her gestures become more and more animated.

Go on, Johnny, go on.

The noise continues. All of a sudden, she brings her hands to her breasts and slides them sensuously down towards her crotch. She rears up.

More, Johnny. Again. Again.

SCENE FOURTEEN

Only the three faces can be seen.

LOLITA

I have a surprise for you, Johnny.

JOHNNY

Fuck, open your legs.

LOLITA

That hurts, Johnny.

GIOVANNI

To Addolorata.

Turn around, *porcocane!*

ADDOLORATA

You woke me up again, Giovanni.

GIOVANNI

Why? Do you want to do it while you're asleep?

ADDOLORATA

You make me sick.

150

JOHNNY-GIOVANNI

To both.

Spread them. Spread your legs. It's not a needle I have here.

LOLITA

It hurts.

JOHNNY

It's normal.

LOLITA

It hurts a lot.

JOHNNY

It's normal.

LOLITA

But why doesn't it hurt you?

JOHNNY

That's normal.

LOLITA AND ADDOLORATA

It hurts me.

JOHNNY-GIOVANNI

What do you want me to do about it? Italian women remain virgins even after ten years of marriage. Move, do something. Here. Here. Pinch me here. Harder. Harder. That doesn't work. That doesn't work either. Get off, I'm going to finish it myself.

He masturbates, his back to the audience.

ADDOLORATA

You always hurt me.

LOLITA

That's not the way I imagined it would be.

JOHNNY

I'll remember my wedding night for a long time. Not even once. My buddy did it fourteen times. If it keeps up like this, it'll take me a year. Not even once. I had to finish it myself.

LOLITA

Cries.

It hurt me. I couldn't.

JOHNNY

If my friends knew, I don't know what I'd do. It wasn't a wedding night, it was a first communion.

LOLITA

Johnny, I've got a surprise for you.

JOHNNY

Hurry up, I feel like sleeping.

He turns his back to the audience.

LOLITA

She takes her guitar and sings "Guantana-mera" in a broken voice.

I would like you to call me Lolita, Johnny. Don't call me Addolorata anymore. Promise me, Johnny?

No answer.

Johnny?

ADDOLORATA

Giovanni?

LOLITA AND ADDOLORATA

You're asleep already?

LOLITA

We're not going to live like our parents, hey Johnny?

The actions of Addolorata and Giovanni suggest that they are in the bedroom. Addolorata's sobs are heard.

GIOVANNI

Waking up.

Porcocane! Still crying? What did I do to you? I should be the one to cry since I had to finish it all alone like a teenager after ten years of marriage. I'm not even allowed that pleasure. I swear, your name suits you! "Addolorata: Our Lady of Sorrows."

ADDOLORATA

It's the only time you touch me. It's the only thing we do together, and you don't even ask for my opinion.

GIOVANNI

Shut up. I need my sleep.

ADDOLORATA

It's the last time. I swear. I swear it's the last time.

> *Lighting fades for a moment. Addolorata holds out her arms to Lolita whose face has drastically changed. They meet in the middle of the stage. To the sound of solemn music, they entwine languorously.*

SCENE FIFTEEN

Addolorata resumes her activity. Long silence.

ADDOLORATA

I'm leaving. I'm going to stay with Maria for awhile.

GIOVANNI

I'm warning you. If you leave, you'll never set foot here again. *Mai più, capito?*

ADDOLORATA

Don't worry. If I leave, I won't be back. You can't understand that. You've never been here long enough to get sick of it.

GIOVANNI

I haven't been living on another planet. I've been living downstairs for the past ten years. You can't say it's paradise. You can't say it's more comfortable down there than it is here. I spend practically twenty hours a day there: from eight in the morning until three o'clock at night. And most of the time I'm just waiting around.

Very loud.

You think I'm not sick of it, selling my bubble gum, a few coffees, cigarettes? You think I'm not sick of it?

ADDOLORATA

If you were really sick of it, you would have done something, you would have changed jobs.

GIOVANNI

Porcocane! Montreal is full of the unemployed and people on welfare. You try to change jobs.

ADDOLORATA

That's not what sickens me the most.

GIOVANNI

Furious.

So say what it is.

Addolorata doesn't answer. Giovanni insists.

Not being rich? You're not the only one. Everyone wants to be rich. But there is one bloody problem: everyone can't be rich at the same time. It's impossible.

ADDOLORATA

That's not what makes me sick. I think that...

She hesitates.

GIOVANNI

Say it. Say what makes you sick. *Dillo, porcocane!*

ADDOLORATA

I think that if we had been less unhappy, we wouldn't have felt as poor as we really were.

156

GIOVANNI

Furious.

Where did you read that? In your pile of *fotoromanzi*?
Or did you hear that on the radio hot line shows? How
do you expect us to be happy with the work you do, the
work I do, with the life we're forced to lead? *Forced!*
You'd have to be an idiot to be happy in our situation,
or else you'd have to start reciting the rosary morning
till night so you could stop thinking. They can't explain
why you're unhappy at mass either.

ADDOLORATA

Mass is the only way out for we Italians... except for
weddings and funerals. It's better than nothing.

GIOVANNI

The next time you see the priest, ask him where the
Providence they teach about in catechism is — the
Providence that's supposed to take care of the poor, like
us.

ADDOLORATA

Ironically.

Maybe it's in the poolroom.

GIOVANNI

Pause.

Remind your priest about the little flowers Providence
was supposed to feed. Did you forget about them? You
have two in the back alley aged eight and nine. They get
more and more wilted because they had the bad luck to
grow in the garden of the poor where there's no sun-
shine. It's always the same ones who get the tools that

Providence gives out. Always the same ones.

ADDOLORATA

I'm going to change my life.

GIOVANNI

How? How are you going to do that?

ADDOLORATA

We weren't able to do it together. I'll try it alone with my children.

GIOVANNI

They're *my* children too!

ADDOLORATA

They won't even notice you're not there. You'll see.

Giovanni, furious, slaps Addolorata.

ADDOLORATA

Impassive. A pause.

You haven't slapped me since my mother's death.

GIOVANNI

They are my children. They are my boys.

Pause.

Those children need their father.

ADDOLORATA

If they were able to get along without him up to now, they'll be able to in the future as well. Didn't we all get along without our fathers while they were here alone? There were thousands...

GIOVANNI

For the past ten years, I've been listening to the old men who spent the fifties here all alone telling me stories they wouldn't tell their wives. Because it's too late. Well, if it's too late for them, it's not too late for me. There's a whole generation of us who spent their childhoods far from their fathers. We are the orphans of immigration. Immigration stole our fathers when we needed them most. That's why we're all fucked up. Don't ask yourself why your father has always been a stranger to you. Don't ask yourself why you could never feel anything for him.

ADDOLORATA

He's always been hard on me.

GIOVANNI

He wasn't given the time to learn not to be hard.

ADDOLORATA

Had we stayed at the *villaggio*, it would have been the same.

GIOVANNI

Do you know what fascism is? They lived it. So that the men could forget their misery, they became little dictators within their own families. And later, they were chased at gunpoint from the land they had cultivated. That's why they emigrated. How can you not be hard on your children when you're convinced that you've emigrated for their sake, that you've abandoned everything you've known for them. He was so terrified that all the sacrifices he made would amount to nothing, that he would never let me do anything other that he knew. It's the same thing for your father. You don't have to look far.

ADDOLORATA

You're a coward. Is that what the alcoholics tell you over the counter in the small hours of the morning? You're all cowards, always wanting to put the blame on someone else. They spend their time yacking. They drink coffee and wine while their wives and children are alone at home. I was as miserable as a dog for ten years with my father and for ten years with you. I've had enough of your emigration stories. Enough. Do you understand? It makes me sick. Those are stories for cowards. Your children wouldn't have seen you any more often even if you hadn't emigrated.

GIOVANNI

Porcocane! You never understand anything. I'm not in any better position than my father. You think the job I do allows me to be better off than my father? I don't know what it means to be a father. How do you want me to know, if my job doesn't allow me to see my children?

Pause.

The only solution you found was to take them away.

160

ADDOLORATA

Don't worry, if the kids need you, they'll come looking
for you.

GIOVANNI

You think they'll come looking for me?

ADDOLORATA

You're worried they won't, right?

GIOVANNI

Yeah, I'm afraid they won't come, because I had to act
with them the way I acted — the only way I could. You
didn't do anything to help. You always made me out to
be a monster, — "Don't do that, I'll tell your father."
Punishment was up to me, you had the rest.

ADDOLORATA

Yes, the rest was for me. But *all* the rest.

GIOVANNI

You, unhappy? And what about what I feel? What do
you call it? When my children fear me, what do you call
that? Is there a word to describe what I feel? Do you
know that word? Do you know it? Do I have to be a
woman to be allowed to admit I'm unhappy?

Almost in tears, he pauses.

I'm unhappy too. You believe I'm the only one to blame
for your unhappiness.

ADDOLORATA

No! no!

GIOVANNI

That's the reason you want to leave me like you left
your father. I... I don't believe that's the reason for our
misery. Everything must be changed. Everything.
Everything.

ADDOLORATA

Moved by her husband's tears.

I can't change everything, Giovanni. I will change what
I can.

She pulls herself together little by little.

I would have liked just to go to school longer, but I
started dreaming in Spanish and finished up in a factory
on Jean-Talon Street. I also ended up with you, and
together we could only make a family worse than those
of our parents. That's what I want to change; that's why
I'm leaving. Our kind of family always manages to
make life as miserable as possible.

GIOVANNI

What's the use of cutting poverty in two. You won't
become any richer for it.

ADDOLORATA

I won't become any poorer either.

GIOVANNI

And if you lose your job?

ADDOLORATA

I've got a safe job.

162

Ironically.

Thanks to you.

GIOVANNI

There are no more safe jobs now.

ADDOLORATA

You won't succeed in scaring me, Giovanni. A person never loses a job that no one wants.

GIOVANNI

Nervously.

So you're really leaving... What did I do that was so bad? There are dozens of women in the district who don't live any better than you. Not one leaves her husband.

ADDOLORATA

Because they're afraid. Because they have no other models. Because there is no woman left in them... their husbands killed everything. They made corpses out of them with nothing left alive inside them since their last pregnancy. Why would they leave? They are as far as they can be from their husbands at home. That's the best place for them to get their revenge, with their closed faces, with their ugly bodies, with their silence. That's the reason they stay.

Long silence.

No, I'll never do that to my children.

GIOVANNI

And me, did you think about me? I don't count. I never counted for anyone. People always leave me without asking me what I think about it. I don't count.

ADDOLORATA

I won't sacrifice myself for anyone anymore, Giovanni. For anyone.

GIOVANNI

Nervously, short of arguments.

Did you think about your father? He just finished burying your mother.

ADDOLORATA

He's going to know that I left him twice in ten years.

GIOVANNI

I don't count, do I? What will I do alone? I need to feel that someone is waiting for me. *Non posso vivere solo.* I can't. I haven't felt like this for twenty years. Addolorata, do you understand? I can't stay alone. *Che faccio solo?* You can't leave. You can't. *Non posso vivere solo.*

Music is heard as an accompaniment to the monologue. Darkness sets.

THE END

SPEAKING WITH AUTHORITY
The Theatre of Marco Micone

The existence of a minority or ethnic voice at the heart of Quebecois literature is rather new. Until recently, the fundamental cleavage between *nous autres* et *les autres* seemed to preclude the possibility of defining the Quebec population and its consciousness in other than dualist terms. Quebec literature, like Quebec scholarly writing, saw only French versus English and hardly recognized the specific existence of the ethnic communities.

If for a very long time the only immigrant culture in Quebec to have produced a significant body of literature was the Jewish community (and it was written in English), this situation is now changing. The Italian and Haitian communities especially, but other groups as well, are beginning to produce works in French which define themselves explicitly within the context of Quebec literature and Quebec society. This process of self-definition accompanies a sudden spurt of interest on the part of Quebec academics (principally sociologists) in the *third constituency* of Quebec society[1]. Such a new perspective will perhaps mark a shift in the role which the *other* communities of Quebec have traditionally been asked to play politically: to neutralize their specificity in aligning themselves with one or the other major group in the province.[2] For many, the increasing visibility and prominence of Quebec's cultural communities promises and end to what has become a sterile stand-off between majority (Francophone) and minority (Anglophone) populations.

Italian writers in Quebec are currently the most visible and active community to emerge during this new phase of cultural readjustment. The recent publication of an anthology of Italian writing in French (*Quêtes*, Guernica Editions, 1983) and the dynamic trans-cultural review *Vice Versa* (a trilingual cultural magazine edited by Italian writers) are indicators of the significant activity of the *Italo-québécois* writers in the cultural life of Quebec.

The work of Marco Micone, playwright and essayist, is of particular interest in this context because of its very explicit social and political focus. Though the representational and somewhat didactic nature of Micone's works sets it apart from much of the writing of other *Italo-québécois* writers — most of whom stay away from explicit references to social and national questions —, Micone shares the concern for language which characterizes much contemporary Quebecois writing.[3] Micone, however, formulates his concern for language within a political universe, a dramatic world informed at all levels by power relationships. Language becomes an instrument and a manifestation of authority. To master language, and this involves mastering particular languages, is to be able to impose one's interpretation of reality.

Micone has written two plays, *Gens du Silence* (translated into English as *Voiceless People*) and *Addolorata*[4]. Both have been successfully produced for Montreal audiences and these plays — along with several essays on immigrant culture — have made Micone the unofficial spokensperson on *minority issues* for the

166

Quebec writer's community. *Voiceless People* is an ambitious fresco which attempts to embrace through the experience of one family the social, political and psychological realities of immigration. Through the story of Antonio — his "expulsion" from his native village, his lonely arrival, his difficult readjustment with his wife and children, his exploitation as a labourer, his steadfast reverence for Authority — and his subsequent conflicts with his wife and daughter, the spectator is given a mass of ideas and opinions about the phenomenon of immigration. The use of symbolic characters, stylized acting, humour and other Brechtian devices provoke a *distancing effect* and introduce mythological elements into the play.

Micone's second play *Addolorata* also uses such devices, but the play focuses particularly on the second-generation immigrants and especially on the relationship between father and daughter, husband and wife. The Authorities which were referred to explicitly in *Voiceless People* (the Church, the Politicians, the Boss) are represented in *Addolorata* mainly through their impact on the power which exercises itself in family relationships.

Though Micone's plays in many ways invite the kind of sociological criticism that ethnic literature has always received, there emerges through the problematic of power and expression a specific nexus of issues. Here the "psychological landscape of ethnic culture" sketched out by Eli Mandel[5] receives its linguistic underpinnings. Certainly one of the principal characteristics of ethnic writing is the sense of linguistic relativity which Daphne Marlatt describes as being characteristic of the world of the immigrant or outsider: "The sensation of having your world turned upside down or inverted also, I think, leads to a sense of the relativity of both language

167

and reality, as much as it leads to a curiosity about other people's realities... It leads to an interest in and curiosity about language, a sense of how language shapes the reality you live in, an understanding of how language is both idiosyncratic (private) and shared (public), and the essential duplicity of language, its capacity to mean several things at once, its figurative and transformational powers."[6] In Micone's plays, this kind of sensitivity is linked, on the one hand, to the status of specific languages (French, English, Italian) within Quebec society and, on the other hand, with the question of the authority of personal expression. Who has the right to speak and what authority will his/her words have?

There is another level at which the relationship between language and authority can be studied with respect to Micone's work and to *Italo-québécois* writing in general. This is the question of the choice of a language of expression by the writer him/herself. Before discussing the dynamics of language and authority in Micone's works, we will situate these same dynamics as they relate to the author's appropriation of a language of expression.

Language Choice and Authorship

The notion of a natural language of expression, dictated only by overwhelming strength of feeling, is a vestige of the Romantic illusion of immediacy. All writers must choose from among the various vernaculars or literary idioms which are offered by their mother tongue. Some writers — members of minority groups or of "minor literatures" — will however, opt for a natural language which is not their own, often because this second language will give them access to a greater readership. Mul-

168

tilingualism has always been treated as a deviation by institutions of criticism, generally formed along national lines. The few odd deviants who have transgressed national barriers and written in second languages (Nabokov, Beckett, Conrad) are treated as singular linguistic acrobats, capable of feats of prowess totally inaccessible to ordinary writers. The writer is by definition a master of his own language; how can he dare attempt to dominate in more than one field?

Writers themselves have been important in reinforcing the notion that there is an exclusive allegiance to the mother tongue. Psychoanalysis, psycho and sociolinguistics have investigated and documented the extremely emotional and exclusive bond between the speaker and his native tongue. But the idea that there is necessarily a mystical union between the writer and a single, native language is false. We have only to consider the huge gap which often existed between the literary language and the vernacular in many cultures. Certain historical eras have sometimes demanded multilingualism for writers: Leonard Forster suggests that during the Renaissance, for example, multilingualism for writers was the rule rather than the exception[7]. Some subjects, for instance, were treated only in specific languages (i.e. love poems in Italian).

In cases where there is the possibility of choice, the use of a particular language for literary expression constitutes what, in the vocabulary of speech-act theory, we could call *appropriateness conditions* for authorship.[8] An author's work will fall into a particular category of discursive practice in part because of the very language, as well of course as the level of language, which has been chosen. One could conceive of the case of a work which conforms in all other ways to the norms of the literary canon of the time, but which would be excluded from the critical arena because of the inappropriateness of its language.

The case of Yiddish in 19th century Europe offers a paradigm for a study of appropriateness conditions relating to the "authorship" of literature.[9] The Jewish writer, generally trilingual, had to choose between Hebrew (the sacred language of the Return to Zion), Yiddish (the "impure jargon" associated with the values of a secular society) and the language of the non-Jewish community. The choice of the writer carried implications which were not only esthetic but also political and social. Before 1830 the term *Yiddish writer* was in fact impossible: Yiddish was considered an unworthy tongue for serious writing, improper for literature. By the beginning of the 20th century, however, Yiddish was the language of a dynamic and modernist literature.

The situation of the Italo-québécois writer in Quebec offers some similarities to that of the 19th century Jewish writer. For the Italo-québécois, Italian is the language of a country and a culture with which he/she is only partially familiar. English is the language of a continent, a powerful and omnipresent trading language. And French, the language of a people whose relationship to the Outsider has yet to be defined. In choosing one of these three languages for literary expression, the writer makes a choice which carries social implications.

In the prefaces to his plays, in the various essays he has written, in his plays themselves, Micone has stated the reasons which led him to choose French as his language of expression.[10] His reasons were political: French is the language which opposes the economic power of *les Anglais* and French is the language which will be understood by those who count: "You can write what you wish, but only if you write in French will we have a chance of being understood and respected for

170

what we are. It's now or never."[11]

Micone was then confronted with an unusual problem however. How to represent the French spoken by Italians when there is no existing, general model to imitate? Micone explains in an interview (*Vice Versa*, February 1984) that after rejecting the idea of a standard, international French and having decided that a popular idiom would not necessarily ridiculize his characters, he opted for a hybrid language. This language, he suggests, represents the street language which Italians will speak in about twenty years from now in Quebec. It is a popular language and includes words like "*Sacraminte*", the Italian version of the popular Quebec swear-word "*Sacrament*".

The somewhat artificially popular, sometimes stylized, nature of language in Micone's plays is one of the elements which sets up a central tension: the conflict between their nature as realistic artefacts, representations of a pre-existing reality, and their nature as interpretation; the play through its very organization imposes on the spectators the "correct" analysis of its contents. By questioning the authority of interpretation of its characters, *Voiceless People* and *Addolorata* lead us to question the authority of the playwright himself. Micone's plays unfold through a dialectic of interpretations, opinion confronting opinion with the clang of crossed swords. Underlying this conflict we sense the playwright's desire to master a complex reality, to use the differing attitudes of the characters to construct a large and complete understanding of immigration in Quebec society. In this endeavour, the language of the playwright — like the words of his characters — is an act whose authority will be "felicitous" because the appropriateness conditions have been met.

The title of Micone's first play, *Gens du Silence*, translated as *Voiceless People* at first seems eminently paradoxical: all of the characters in Micone's plays talk a lot. They talk too much in fact, and their very volubility becomes suspect as the play proceeds. Too many words can begin to sound like silence when we realize that words can be used not only to convey information or to express emotion but also to indicate self-importance — or to mask the fear of nothingness.

But words are also interpretations of reality and the talking matches in Micone's plays are jousts, conflicting versions of reality which confront one another in mutual incomprehension. There are basically three voices in these discussions: that of the dominant male (Antonio, Giovanni) who represents the traditional, conservative view; that of the subordinate but lucid female (Anna, Nancy, Addolorata) perhaps on her way to emancipation; that of the symbolic character, Zio in *Voiceless People* and the announcer in *Addolorata*. The male-female voices confront one another in dialectic; the symbolic characters introduce a third voice, a synthesis giving the play larger dimensions. We see language operating as an instrument of power within the family (who speaks, what authority do his/her words have) and also as an indicator of social status. Because languages in Quebec are identified with different social constituencies, we are given through the characters in the plays an often humorous version of the immigrant's perception of these associations.

For Antonio, English is the language of the bosses and therefore the language which inspires respect. Antonio insists therefore that his children go to school in English. "Ya, the English not only have all the right cards, they know how to play them too. That's why they win. It's important to understand that. Not for us, it's too late for us. But for the children. They have to learn how to win. That's why we have to send them to English school." Nancy will retort at the end of the play, however: "It's not the language that makes the boss."

Antonio's son, Mario, who was born in Quebec and who did indeed go to English school, speaks half-French and half-English and copiously punctuates the resulting mixture with *fuck*'s. Antonio is proud that Mario can speak three languages, but Mario's unsure grip on language is a reflection of his inability to obtain social advancement, he will go to work in the same factory as his father. He is consoled by the marvellous roar of his Trans-Am.

Lolita, the young fiancée in *Addolorata*, sees only advantages in multilingualism. Her "four languages" are a precious asset for *marriagiability* and the good life: "With my four languages I can watch the soap operas in English, read the T.V. Hebdo in French and the photo-novellas in Italian, and sing *Guantanamera*.»

Satire here reveals the link between a profusion of languages and cultural poverty. Possessing language is not only manipulating a code correctly, and in many cases of multilingualism, especially among immigrants, this level of mastery is often not attained. Language and culture are the means through which individuals interpret their past and their present. The incapacity to master language becomes, in *Voiceless People*, the inability to understand one's reality. Nancy: "I teach adolescents who have Italian names and whose only culture is that of silence. Silence on the peasant origins of their parents. Silence on the reasons which led their parents to emigrate. Silence on the manipulations of which they are victims. Silence on the country in which they live and on

173

the reasons for this silence.»

The counterpart to these silences are the certainties of Antonio, the convictions he uses to protect himself from nothingness. Antonio is for Authority, against the Separatists, for his wife staying at home, for the English, for the Church and its processions. Antonio believes that French-Canadians are lazy, and that hard work must be accompanied by respect for those who command. "Here we only need strong men to defend what we have and to protect respect for authority."

Antonio's knowledge has been gathered through suffering and work. When his ideas are challenged, he maintains that his view of reality is the only valid one because supported on this foundation. Nancy articulates the relationship between authorized opinion and status when she says sarcastically: "You can understand because you're neither young nor a woman." Antonio has dedicated his life to the building of this edifice of conviction just as he has sacrificed himself for the acquisition of a house. This house, detested by Mario as a useless museum and by Nancy as the symbol of all the privations the children have suffered because of it, is for Antonio tangible compensation for the loss he has suffered as an immigrant. "Here I have no ancestors to protect me/Here I have no hills to surround me/For an immigrant, the house is more than a house."

In *Addolorata* Johnny/Giovanni also attempts to impose his vision of reality on his wife. Johnny and Lolita are second-generation immigrants (or they have immigrated at an early age). Johnny differs from Antonio in his more complex and radical view of immigration. This difference is economically justified in the play by the fact that Johnny has refused to work for a boss, choosing instead to run a pool room. His clients are "educated people", "on our side". Giovanni's critiques

174

of capitalist economy are radical: "If emigration were a good thing, it would not have been left to poor people like us and our parents..."; "In a country where the rich and the bosses lead the government by the nose, all the poor, all the workers are immigrants, even if their names are Tremblay or Smith.»

In *Addolorata* the historical and economic explanations of the immigrant condition begin to sound like rhetoric. Giovanni does not hear Addolorata when she says that she does not want to have a boss either and that she is leaving him. Giovanni is convinced that Addolorata understands nothing. "You think that the only cause of all your unhappiness is me... That's why you want to leave me just like you left your father. Me, I think that the cause of our misery is not to be found here. Everything must change. Everything." But Addolorata refuses the political argument and returns to the personal: "I can't change everything, Giovanni. But I will change whatever I can."

In Micone's plays, then, male rhetoric is an active agent in the oppression of women. In the dialectic of power/powerlessness which characterizes the particular situation of the male immigrant (source of authority within the family, powerless outside the home) rhetoric — whether it be from the right or the left — becomes an almost concrete manifestation of selfhood. Conflicting interpretations, as presented by Nancy and by Addolorata, are quite simply unacceptable within the context of the family and the couple. Their words do not carry the necessary weight. Though Gino, Nancy's comrade in agitation, can remain within Chiuso (the Italian community) to pursue his goals, Nancy cannot. She must attempt to find some place outside where she might perhaps find words which will be heard.

If Micone the playwright can choose from among

various languages of expression the one most appropriate to his needs, his characters have little choice. Although Antonio lives the illusion of control, he shows himself to be a victim of language. Antonio remains trapped within a net of illusion which keeps him from the authenticity associated with his daughter Nancy. Is this authenticity also an illusion? Do Nancy and Addolorata have a privileged relationship to language precisely because of their very powerlessness? This indeed seems to be the dialectic presented by Micone: the language of authenticity is accessible only to those excluded from the possibilities of both power (economic power) and authority (the limited power exercised by the head of the family). Because they are *doubly immigrant*, women have no stake in and no access to the rhetoric of authority.

By adopting the family as his particular area of investigation, by shattering questions of language and power into a dynamic configuration of interrelated fragments, Micone shows finally that the "immigrant question" is simply a variant of the theme of powerlessness. Here is a subject, suggests Micone, on which women speak with authority.

NOTES

1. Both *Sociologie et sociétés* (Vol. XV, no. 2, Oct., 83) and *Recherches sociographiques* (February, 1985) have recently brought out issues on ethnicity in Quebec. The Institut québécois de recherche sur la culture has made the question of ethnicity one of its priority areas of research and has produced an impressive number of publications over the last few years, for example: *Les Juifs du Québec*, bibliographie rétrospective annotée, David Rome *et al.* (1981); *La communauté grecque du Québec*, Tina Ioannou (1984). See also *Spirale*, décembre 1983, for a dossier on "Écriture et minorités au Québec".

2. "The only choice we've been given is to make what we are 'converge' with what they are, the better to be suffocated by the weight of the majority" (*Gens du Silence*).

3. See Fulvio Caccia's article in this issue on Italian poets in Quebec.

4. Marco Micone, *Gens du Silence*, Québec/Amérique, 1982. Published in English translation, *Voiceless People* (tr. Maurizia Binda), Guernica Edition, 1984. *Addolorata*, Guernica, 1984. Published in part in *Quêtes*, Guernica Edition, 1983. "Propos d'enfants", *Dérives* 17-18 (1979), pp. 20-25. "La culture immigrée", *Dérives* 29-30 (1981) pp. 87-93.

5. Eli Mandel, "The Ethnic Voice in Canadian writing", *Another Time*, Press Porcépic, 1977, p. 92.

6. Daphne Marlatt, "Entering in" the Immigrant Imagination. *Canadian Literature*. Anniversary issue, pp. 219-223.

7. Leonard Forster, *The Poet's Tongues. Multilingualism in Literature*. Cambridge University Press, 1970.

8. For the questions of authorship and appropriateness conditions, see: Michel Foucault, "What is an Author?" in *Language, Counter-Memory, Practice*. Selected Essays and Interviews. Ed. Donald F. Bouchard. Trans. D.F. Bouchard and S. Simon. Cornell University Press, 1977, and Mary Louise Pratt, *Towards a Speech Act Theory of Literature*. Bloomington: Indiana University Press, 1971.

9. Régine Robin's excellent book *L'amour du yiddish: écriture et sentiment de la langue, 1830-1930* (Éditions du Sorbier, Paris, 1983) is a precious source of information on this question.

10. See Micone's essays indicated in note 2. It is interesting to note that Micone, like many new immigrants in the 50s, was refused entry to French school. Very paradoxically he learned French at McGill. One of the major consequence of law 101 in Quebec has been that one out of five children at French school now is of other than French-Canadian origin. (See *Le Devoir*, supplement on the cultural communities, Sept 1984). Of the eighteen writers published in *Quêtes*, an anthology of *Italo-québécois* writing, all but seven of the contributions were originally written in French. (Five in English, two in Italian.)

11. The translations are mine as the English version of the play was not yet available at the time of writing.

By the Same Author

Gens du silence (1982)
Addolorata (1984)
Déjà l'agonie (1988)